THE MEDIÆVAL STYLES OF THE ENGLISH PARISH CHURCH

A Survey of their Development, Design and Features

BY

F. E. HOWARD

Joint Author of " English Church Woodwork during the Mediæval Period "

Illustrated from Photographs

LONDON
B. T. BATSFORD LTD.
15 NORTH AUDLEY STREET, W.1

First Published, Autumn 1936

MADE AND PRINTED IN GREAT BRITAIN
FOR THE PUBLISHERS, B. T. BATSFORD
LTD., BY THE DARIEN PRESS, EDINBURGH

PREFACE

WHEN Sir William St. John Hope died in 1919, the only man living to compare with him in knowledge of ecclesiastical art in the Middle Ages was the young archæologist who has all too soon followed him. St. John Hope's position and circumstances made it natural and easy for him to impart a goodly share of his vast stores of information to other students ; F. E. Howard's large and ever-growing practice as an ecclesiastical architect allowed him little leisure to arrange for publication the fruits of his research. At his death in the Spring of 1934, at the early age of 45, much of his learning perished with him, or survived only in the minds of those who knew him and had learned to look upon him as the unfailing source of information on any question of mediæval art.

But he left among his papers the MS. of a book on Local Variations of Style in English Parish Churches, upon which he had been working for many years. The first part, at least, of this, a survey of the architectural development of the Parish Church, was in such an advanced stage of preparation that though its editors may feel, with Shakespeare's, " it had been a thing worthy to have been wished that the Author himself had lived to have set forth and overseen his own writings," they yet believe that it represents, in the words of one well qualified to judge, " a lucid, careful, but not too detailed nor technical study of the development of style and design in the Parish Churches of England, largely founded upon first-hand observation of examples in every part of the country ; combining the older chronological approach of Bloxam and Parker with the analytical method of Bond, and informed throughout with the results of recent scholarship in the domain of documentary evidence."

As such, illustrated by the full resources of modern photography, it is presented to the large and increasing public now interested in English antiquities, including that which is learning to use the motor car not as a pastime but as, perhaps, the most valuable means of recreation and culture that this mechanical age has produced.

There is reason to hope that the second part of the MS., a study of local variations of style determined by geographical and economic conditions, may also be found to be sufficiently complete to form a complementary volume for publication at a later date under the title " Local Types in the English Parish Church."

E. A. GREENING LAMBORN.

OXFORD, *October* 1936.

Students and architects, and indeed all lovers
of the beautiful, owe a great debt of gratitude to
Mr E. A. Greening Lamborn for his work in
seeing this present volume of my husband's
through the press.

YVONNE HOWARD.

ACKNOWLEDGMENT

THE publishers must acknowledge their obligation to the photographers whose work is represented in these pages, namely, the late Dr. Granville Buckley for Figs. 13, 18, 65, 71, 84-87, 89, 92, 93, 121, 128, 135 and 150 (from the collection of the Courtauld Institute of Art, University of London) ; the late Mr. B. C. Clayton for Figs. 1, 2, 5-9, 14-16, 20, 22-25, 27, 29-36, 38, 39, 42-46, 50, 54-60, 61, 66, 69, 77, 79, 80, 82, 88, 91, 95, 97, 99, 100, 103, 106, 117, 118, 122, 130, 147, 153, 154, 158, 159, 169, 171, 173, 176, 178 and 180 ; Mr. F. H. Crossley, F.S.A., for Figs. 19, 21, 49, 73, 74, 81, 83, 94, 101, 104, 105, 111, 116, 124-126, 131, 133, 137, 138, 148, 151, 157, 162-164, 166, 167 and 172 ; the late Mr. De Ath (of Leominster), for Fig. 112 ; Messrs. F. Frith & Co. Ltd. for Figs. 62, 63, 98 and 109 ; Mr. P. Goodchild for Figs. 115 and 136 ; Mr. E. A. Greening Lamborn for Figs. 67 and 68 ; Mr. C. E. Hodges for Figs. 51 and 52 ; the late Mr. F. E. Howard for Figs. 4, 72, 90, 102, 113, 127, 129, 132, 140, 144, 145, 149, 165, 168, 170, 175 and 179; Mr. T. E. Routh for Figs. 53, 114 and 160 ; the late Rev. F. Sumner for Figs. 3, 10-12, 28, 64, 107, 110, 134 (top subject), 143, 146, 152, 174 and 177 ; Mr. Will F. Taylor for Figs. 17, 40, 41, 134 (bottom subject), 139 and 141 ; Messrs. J. Valentine & Sons for Fig. 76. Figs. 26, 37, 47, 48, 70, 75, 78, 96, 108, 119, 120, 123, 142, 155, 156 and 161 are from the Publishers' collections.

CONTENTS

CHAP.   PAGE

PREFACE v

I. INTRODUCTION 1

II. HINTS ON THE STUDY OF CHURCH DEVELOPMENT 7

III. BEGINNINGS OF THE SAXON STYLE 16

IV. THE LATER PRE-CONQUEST STYLE 24

V. THE TRANSITION FROM SAXON TO NORMAN 31

VI. THE NORMAN STYLE 35

VII. THE TRANSITION FROM NORMAN TO EARLY ENGLISH . . . 51

VIII. THE EARLY ENGLISH STYLE 57

IX. THE TRANSITION FROM EARLY ENGLISH TO DECORATED . . . 65

X. THE DECORATED STYLE 69

XI. THE TRANSITION FROM DECORATED TO PERPENDICULAR . . . 76

XII. THE PERPENDICULAR STYLE 79

BRIEF GLOSSARY OF ARCHITECTURAL TERMS 89

INDEX UNDER COUNTIES 92

GENERAL INDEX 96

THE MEDIÆVAL STYLES OF THE ENGLISH PARISH CHURCH

CHAPTER I

INTRODUCTION

THIS age of mechanical science has done us at least one good turn. It has enabled us to rediscover the delights of the countryside. Though the car, the bus and the motor coach are rapidly destroying the beauty of the main roads by the hideous trail of shoddy bungalows, roadside advertisements and petrol stations which inevitably spring up on their track, they have brought the town-dweller into closer touch with the country than the railways ever did. One of the results of this invasion of the country by the town is that the village church, which plays such a large part in the English landscape, is receiving more attention than ever before, even at the height of the Gothic Revival, or when a smattering of architectural knowledge was an essential part of polite education. Often when photographing in an old church I have been amazed and sometimes inconvenienced by the stream of hot cyclists and opulent motorists who invade the quiet building. Most of these are mere sightseers, often a little bewildered by their unfamiliar surroundings, but very many evidently find a real pleasure in the simple, serene beauty of it all. Very few know anything of mediæval architecture, or can read the history plainly written on the walls, yet there is certainly a widespread desire to know more about it. I meet many people to whom architecture is a great joy, but who realise that a little more knowledge would increase their pleasure tenfold. These often ask me to tell them of some simple book on the subject. Now books on the English churches are numerous indeed, and very many have issued from the press just lately, but I do not know of one which, by itself, would give an appreciative but ignorant student a clear idea of the evolution and character of English church architecture. Most of them assume that the reader already knows a good deal about the subject. Some are too technical, some too superficial, others insufficiently illustrated. Several of the best are out of print and extremely costly. Almost all, by including the great cathedrals and abbeys, attempt to cover too much ground. There seems to be a real need for a book which does not assume any previous knowledge on the part of the reader, dealing only with simple parish churches, treating the development

A   I

of mediæval architecture, not as a series of capricious changes of fashion but as a gradual and logical evolution of the art of church building. It is no use at an early stage to confuse the mind of the student by attempting to deal with the great cathedral and monastic churches, with their complicated planning and design and elaborate detail. The wise inquirer will start on the simpler buildings and leave the more ambitious structure for future delight. A thorough acquaintance with the parish church is the best basis for a real understanding and appreciation of the cathedrals.

The learner is often appalled by technical terms, surely unnecessarily. When errand boys talk glibly of induction and capacity, anode-bend rectification and low-frequency amplification, surely those possessed of more than an elementary school education should not shy at jambs and mullions, clerestories or tracery. Technical terms are intended to simplify a subject, not to complicate it. I intend to use as few as possible, but space alone forbids the employment of a dozen words of ordinary usage where one technical term would suffice.

With an elementary but sound knowledge of architecture, church hunting is an enthralling pursuit. No church should be passed without entering it, for some apparently modern and uninviting structures will often be found to retain some trace of a former and more beautiful building, even if it be but a font or a tomb.

The interest will be much increased if some record is made of the visit. A camera affords the means of fixing in the memory details which would otherwise be forgotten. A pencil and sketchbook are even better, though it is to be feared that few can spare the time for sketching in these restless days. For those who neither photograph nor sketch, the village post-office or general store can generally supply photographic postcards, often passably good, as memoranda. A notebook is also useful in which to jot down those points of interest which appeal to us, or failing this, notes and corrections may be made in the margin of the inevitable " Little Guide," but without some sort of record, except in rare cases of abnormal memory, details will eventually fade from the recollection. A collection of postcards, still more of photographs taken by oneself, will prove a great joy on winter days when further excursions are out of the question ; and much may be learnt by comparison of church with church, and details studied which could not be properly examined on our visit.

Those who take their own photographs can increase their collection by exchange with other enthusiasts, and may thus come to know of interesting buildings neglected by the guidebooks. There are also a few postal photographic clubs which circulate portfolios of architectural photographs, and these afford an excellent means of learning of fresh and little-known subjects and better methods of photography.

The subject is one which appeals to a variety of types of mentality. Those whose interest is purely artistic may rest content with the enjoyment

2   BRIXWORTH, NORTHAMPTONSHIRE, LOOKING WEST :   a once-aisled Saxon fabric of the seventh century

3 THE AISLED LATE NORMAN NAVE OF WALSOKEN, NORFOLK

of the beauty of an old church, the charm of its proportion, the details of moulding and carving, the varied colour and texture of its masonry and roofing. Those of a more scientific turn of mind may experience some of the satisfaction of a skilled detective searching for clues, in analysing the periods of the building and attempting to reconstruct its history. To others the religious side may make the strongest appeal, and these may rejoice over the survivals of the old order, and the few successful modern efforts to restore a building to its former glory, or may sigh over the wanton destruction by iconoclasts or by zealous but ignorant restorers.

To some, mediæval architecture will be but an interesting survival of the past, a method of building now superseded. Others will realise that it contains the germ of everything beautiful, from which the architecture of the future will spring, perhaps centuries hence, when the present cult of the ugly, the bizarre, the gaunt, the mechanical, shall have passed away.

A mediæval parish church may be a magnificent pile (17, 96, 111, 140) or a very humble affair (20, 35, 42), but it is always beautiful and interesting, provided it has not been spoilt by clumsy modern alterations. The mediæval builders had an unerring sense of proportion and feeling for scale, and seemed to know exactly what could be done with the means and materials at their disposal. Mediæval building is, before all things, reasonable building. Compared with the architect of to-day the old master craftsman was an unlearned and ignorant man. He knew nothing of former styles, nor did he yearn to invent new ones, but he had a thorough knowledge of the practice of his own day and was always seeking to improve upon it, though he did not deliberately attempt to be original. Generation after generation of craftsmen felt their way gradually towards the ideal church, never straining, never hurrying, but progressing always.

In the art history of the world there have been several periods of high achievement, each preceded by an age of experiment and followed by a speedy decline. Most of our parish churches were built between the years 1000 and 1550, and during these five hundred and fifty years a method of building, far superior to any which had gone before, was gradually developed all over Western Europe, attained its greatest perfection, and within a few decades was a thing of the past. England was a comparatively small and insignificant country on the borders of the civilised world, and only an exaggerated sense of insular superiority could lead one to expect to find the origins of the style in our own land ; yet the mediæval builders of England were closely in touch with Continental progress and took their fair share in the series of architectural experiments which were being made throughout western Christendom. They kept well abreast of Continental practice and at some periods they were distinctly ahead of their rivals.

The mediæval architecture of England sprang from the ruins of the Romano-British civilisation.

Of Romano-British churches we know practically nothing, though it is just possible that remains of one are incorporated in the chancel of St. Martin's at Canterbury, and the foundations of at least two others, at Silchester and Caerleon, have been excavated within recent years.

There are several churches standing, and foundations of others, dating from the period of St. Augustine's mission (597), and these are to all intents and purposes Romano-British rather than Anglo-Saxon in plan and style.

The Danish raids caused a remarkably complete destruction of Christian churches. A very few buildings may be tentatively assigned to the brief interlude of peace during the reign of Alfred and his immediate successors, but there is very little evidence to show how the old tradition was kept alive, as it certainly was, until with the final Danish Conquest followed an era of peace and the conversion of the conquerors.

Church building then went on apace and developed rapidly into a distinct style. From that time onwards architecture was continually changing and improving. New fashions and methods spread rapidly, not only over the whole of England but all over Western Europe. The change and development were continuous, but moved much more rapidly at some periods than at others. Consequently it is possible to distinguish several distinct styles appertaining to those years when development slowed down for a while. Names, quite arbitrary and inappropriate but useful because generally understood and accepted, have been assigned by modern antiquaries to these styles : pre-Conquest, Norman, Early English, Decorated, and Perpendicular. The intermediate periods during which development was more rapid are known as Transition Norman, Transition Early English to Decorated, and so on.

Some more knowledgeable persons may take exception to my employment of the old nicknames, preferring the recent practice of naming by centuries. Admittedly they are nicknames, very inaptly chosen, having no relation whatever to the styles they purport to describe, but they have been in use for over a century and are generally understood. Some archæologists have even asserted that development was so continuous and uniform that no division into styles is possible. Facts are against them. Development indeed was continuous, but not uniform, and it is rare to find a feature which cannot be immediately assigned to one of the recognised styles or to one of the shorter periods of transition. I have tried and abandoned the system of classification by centuries. It is thoroughly unsound. Unfortunately, though one of the periods of transition occurred conveniently at the end of a century, the others all took place in the middle. To take concrete examples from my own city, Oxford, the term thirteenth century covers buildings of such widely differing style as the parish church of St. Giles and the chapel of Merton College, while fourteenth century must include such totally different decorative systems as those employed in the Latin Chapel of the Cathedral and New College chapel. Again, the Perpendicular style refused to be confined within the limits of a century and flourished for over two hundred years, lingering on till the present day. The Perpendicular style is unmistakable, but he is a bold man who would assign a definite century to a building of this style without other confirmatory evidence.

No. Rickman and his contemporaries showed a remarkable lack of imagination in the bestowal of these nicknames, but they stuck, because, like most nicknames, they are convenient.

THE BUILDERS. Who were the men that built our parish churches? The common notion seems to be that they were the monks, and another very prevalent belief is that in the old days men worked for the love of it, without hope of reward. It has been definitely proved that both of these popular ideas are wrong. Professed monks only very rarely engaged in the building craft, and then only in their own abbeys. The parish churches were built by paid craftsmen who quite evidently loved their work, but certainly would not have taken such pleasure in it without the prospect of pay-day.

Two systems seem to have been in use then as now, namely direct labour and the contract system, and it is evident that the contract system became more and more general as the Middle Ages drew to a close, though the other system still survived.

By the method of direct labour, which probably prevailed in earlier times, the employer provided the material, engaged workmen and a master craftsman to oversee the actual construction, and paid each item of the expense separately. A surveyor or clerk of the works might be called in to deal with the engagement of workmen, the collection of material and the payment of wages. It was the master craftsman who drew up the necessary plans to suit the requirements of the employer.

By the method of contract, the employer would approach a master craftsman, who would provide the design and undertake to complete the building for a definite sum, or at least that portion of the building with which his particular trade was concerned, for there were usually separate contracts for each trade. Thus it was usual to employ a master mason to complete the foundations, walls and floors, and then a master carpenter contracted to roof the building. This explains why the roofs of some churches seem to be designed with little or no relation to the openings and piers of the walls which support them. The system of separate contracts for each trade still survives in the North of England, but is fast dying out. It will be seen how it enabled each craftsman to concentrate on his particular craft, while the architect of to-day must have at least a theoretical knowledge of all the crafts, which few ordinary brains are capable of grasping.

In the Middle Ages the designing of a building was part of the duties of a master craftsman. The modern architect corresponds most nearly to the surveyor of works, and has taken upon himself the design of the building, once the prerogative of the master craftsman. One of the reasons why mediæval buildings please us so much is that they were designed by the men who built them, men who were used not only to drawing architectural forms, but familiar with working them in the actual stone or wood.

Many building accounts have survived showing how the direct labour system actually worked, for instance those for building the chancel of Adderbury Church, the south transept of Thame or the Steeple of Louth (7), not to mention innumerable fabric rolls of the cathedrals and abbeys. And mediæval contracts are perhaps equally numerous.

A mediæval contract was often a very complete document, combining with the undertaking to complete the building for a stated sum, to be paid at stated times, a clear description of the structure and often a fairly detailed specification. Such are the contracts for Fotheringhay Church, Northamptonshire; Catterick Church, Yorkshire; a chapel added to St. Mary's, Chester; and for a church house at Sherston, Wiltshire.

It was a very usual custom for the employer to supply a part at least of the material, and this is frequently mentioned in ancient contracts.

Towards the end of our period it is certain that much masonry was worked at the quarries and supplied ready for fixing in buildings perhaps many miles distant. This is most evident in the West Country, where there is very good reason to suppose that arcades and windows in beerstone were worked at some centre and supplied to churches for many miles round, while Ham Hill windows and arcades seem to have been sent from one or two large workshops not only over South Somerset and Dorset, but even to South Wales. On the other hand, while most of the stone used in Norfolk came from Northamptonshire, there is not the slightest trace of the Northamptonshire masoncraft in the churches of that county, which proves that the system did not hold good in this district. One of the earliest instances of stone being worked at a centre instead of on the site is found in the working of Purbeck marble, where the local workshops carried on their trade in true modern commercial fashion, supplying turned shafts, fonts, tombs and effigies to clients in very distant parts.

In fact, the conditions in the building trade were not very different in the Middle Ages from those of the present day. Human nature has changed very little in the course of six hundred years or so. Church building then was not very different from church building now, except in the all-important fact that then the designer was a practical builder who worked at his trade; now he is a professional man, a theorist, only partially in touch with the trades which he attempts to direct.

4 WEST WALTON: a rich Early English church of the Norfolk Marshland

5 THE SOUTH NAVE AISLE OF PATRINGTON, YORKSHIRE:
a fine cruciform Decorated church

CHAPTER II

HINTS ON THE STUDY OF CHURCH DEVELOPMENT

IT is very little use to attempt to study the architectural history of a church in detail before having seen some of the neighbouring churches. It is very usual to find that the development of some of these has proceeded on similar lines, but has been arrested at an earlier stage. It is quite likely that a church may be found which has never been altered since its first building. This will often give a good idea of the original nucleus around which the church you are studying has grown. Each district seems to have had its favourite methods of enlargement and the expedients common in one part of the country are exceptional, or even unknown, in other regions.

It is useful to remember that the earliest portions likely to survive are the two eastern angles of the nave. The east wall of the nave formed the boundary between the portion of the fabric for which the parishioners were responsible and that whose upkeep was the duty of the rector, and it seems in most cases to have escaped total rebuilding in consequence. Perhaps the two western angles of the nave are the next most likely places to find traces of the earliest building, and then the side walls, over the arcades, if these should be earlier than 1300. Original work in the chancel seems to have had far less chance of survival, since chancels were so often not only lengthened but also widened in later times. The western portions of the side walls are more likely to retain original portions than the eastern, owing to the later fashion of eastward extension.

It may be well to caution the investigator against an error very dear to the heart of the compiler of guidebooks. So many, finding the earliest architectural features in an aisle, propound the theory that the aisle was the original nave and that the present nave has been added at the side. Instances of this do occur, for instance at Westhall, Alton and Charlwood, but they are exceedingly rare. The chances are about four hundred to one that the main east and west axis of the church has never changed in spite of successive enlargements and additions to every part of the fabric.

Another frequent source of error is to assume that the church originally consisted of a nave only, or a chancel without a nave. It was not the custom to build portions of churches and leave the completion to future generations. There may be exceptions, but it is safe to say that the average parish church was originally built as a complete whole.

It is easy enough for even a beginner to judge the approximate date of a window or doorway, but it is far more difficult to say to what period the

7

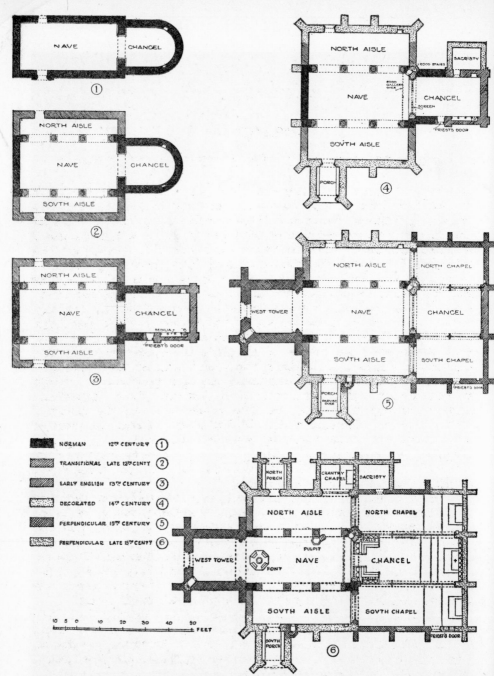

COMPARATIVE PLANS OF THE DEVELOPMENT OF A TYPICAL PARISH CHURCH
DURING THE MEDIÆVAL PERIODS.

(1) Norman ; nave and apsidal chancel. ·
(2) Transitional ; narrow aisles added.
(3) Early English ; chancel lengthened and end squared.
(4) Decorated ; aisles widened, south porch and sacristy added.
(5) Perpendicular ; west tower added and aisles prolonged to form chancel chapels.
(6) Late Perpendicular ; chancel and chancel aisles lengthened, porch and chantry chapel added on north sid

From diagrams prepared by Arthur Stratton, F.S.A., F.R.I.B.A., and Geoffry Lucas, F.S.A., F.R.I.B.A.

8

6 THE NAVE ARCADES OF THE GREAT FIFTEENTH-CENTURY
"WOOL" CHURCH OF CIRENCESTER, GLOUCESTERSHIRE

7 A GRACEFUL LATE FIFTEENTH-CENTURY SPIRE: Louth, Lincolnshire

actual walling belongs. Windows and doorways were so often inserted in older walls that they cannot be relied upon as evidence for the date of the wall. The type of masonry is a help to a right decision, but the best evidence is the design of the base course (170) or the string course, if the wall possesses these features. Their absence in some districts is a mark of early date. Buttresses were often added to strengthen an older wall and are less reliable indications, unless the base course passes round them.

The method of investigation favoured by some sound antiquaries is to strip the building of its later features, period by period, doing in the abstract what some of the more iconoclastic nineteenth-century restorers did in actuality, until at last they arrive at the original structure.

In studying the development of a church it is all-important to find the nucleus around which it has developed, but it is possible to overrate the intrinsic value of early work. The reason why the original church has been altered and enlarged was that it was inadequate for the needs of succeeding generations and failed to satisfy their sense of beauty or their notions of good craftsmanship. Alterations were made for good reasons. Generally every addition has increased not only its beauty and dignity but its practical utility. Those who grumble at the incongruity of large windows in a Norman nave should remember that with the original tiny lights the early carving they admire would have been lost in gloom.

It is exceptional to find beautiful early work spoilt by later development. An instance of this is the wonderful thirteenth-century church of West Walton (4, 82) in Norfolk, ruined by the later addition of excessively wide aisles. The mediæval builders had no respect for antiquity as such, and had no hesitation in destroying the beautiful work of their predecessors, confident that what they were substituting was far more beautiful. And they were usually justified in this belief. Every addition seems to increase the loveliness of a mediæval church and to add to its interest, giving it something of the fascination of a living creature.

It is a question whether the interior or the exterior should be inspected first. Most authorities say the outside. Personally, in spite of E. A. Freeman's famous dictum that no one but a fool enters a church without first inspecting the exterior, unless the church is aisleless, I start my investigations with the interior, since that is where the oldest portions are likely to be found.

Having entered the church and taken up a position in the nave, look first at the arcades. If these start some distance from the end walls it is likely that the wall they support is earlier. If the two arcades are of different dates, that again is evidence for the earlier date of the nave walls, and if the arches seem to be older than 1300 it is very likely that old walling has been retained in the spandrels above them. Note if there are any remains of the old side windows of the nave in these spandrels, either towards the nave or towards the aisles. It is quite likely that you will find some indications of Norman windows, or even work of pre-Conquest date, and on the side towards the aisle you may find traces of pilaster strips, as at Bibury, Gloucestershire, or flat Norman buttresses, as at Cuddesdon, Oxfordshire, or the old corbel table, as at Farmington, Gloucestershire. If there are no indications of the date of the nave walls inside, it may be well to go outside and see whether the original quoins of the nave are visible. These may be hidden or destroyed by the later addition of a west tower or a subsequent enlargement of the chancel, but in all probability you will find traces of them. If these go down to ground level there is certain evidence that the nave was originally aisleless, and therefore earlier than the arcades. The character of the quoining may decide whether it is Norman or pre-Conquest. If of very small stones a Norman date may usually be inferred. If of very large and irregular stones a fairly early pre-Conquest fabric is indicated (20), while long and short work (22, 24) is a sign that the original aisleless nave was built some time between 950 and 1066.

It is worth while to examine the responds of the nave arcade (85), especially if they do not correspond with the pillars. They may belong to an earlier arcade, and they often show by a change in the character of the masonry of the upper part that the earlier arcade was much lower. Sometimes the old capital has been left in position, some feet below the present one.

If the chancel arch is much out of the centre it is probable that the nave has been widened on one side or the other, and that the original nave wall on that side has been destroyed. In rare cases, as at Beaudesert, the nave has been reduced in width, also resulting in the destruction of the earlier work.

The chancel arch may, or may not, be part of the first building. Very many early examples have been left unaltered, while some, though the arch is later, have preserved the old jambs ; but the enlarging of the chancel arch was one of the commonest of mediæval alterations. A chancel arch of fourteenth or fifteenth century style is no evidence against the early date of the nave. Naves were often enlarged by lengthening. If there are but two or three arches on each side this is not likely to have taken place, but if there are five or more, and particularly if the nave looks unduly long, it is well to look for signs of the alteration. Often there is a portion of the old side wall of the nave left between the older arcade and the more recent work, and often there is an obvious change in the detail. But sometimes the whole arcade has been renewed from east to west, and there is no visible sign of any break. In this case the only thing left to be done is to look for a change of design, such as an alteration in the section or level of the base course, in the wall of one or both the aisles.

The extension of the nave eastwards was one of the most uncommon of all methods of enlargement, since it meant encroaching on the domain of the rector, the curtailing of the chancel at its west end, and hence the

8 QUIET MIDLAND PERPENDICULAR: South Newington, Oxfordshire

9 BISHOP'S CLEEVE, GLOUCESTERSHIRE: a large Norman cruciform fabric

lengthening of the chancel eastwards. In a case of this sort there will sometimes be signs of the earlier chancel arch—perhaps its responds, or a plain piece of walling between the earlier and later portions of the arcade. If there are traces of a rood-loft stairway more than one bay from the east end of the nave, as at Little Walsingham, Norfolk, it is reasonable to suppose that an eastward extension has taken place, even if the design of the arcade is uniform throughout.

It is sometimes found that the arcade terminates in a half arch at one of its extremities, and that is certain evidence that the original proportions of the nave have been curtailed. This may be due to several causes. The most uncommon is the extension of the chancel westwards. Less unusual, but still very uncommon, is the later building of a central tower at the east end of the nave, as at Willersey, Gloucestershire. But the shortening of the nave by building a west tower inside instead of outside the west wall, is a very common alteration indeed, particularly when the position of the church is close to the graveyard boundary at the west end.

The clerestory is most likely to be a later addition, unless it is obvious that the details are contemporary with the arcades, and that these are certainly not insertions. It is worth while to look carefully for traces of earlier clerestory windows below or between the present windows, for often an early clerestory was heightened in later times, or a new clerestory built above an earlier one, particularly if a later widening and raising of the aisles had rendered the old one useless. If the clerestory is simply a heightening of a former low structure some trace of the former windows is quite likely to remain, for the old custom was to set these over the piers, while in later work they were usually over the apex of the arches. For instance, the old circular windows of the fourteenth-century clerestories remain between and below the larger fifteenth-century windows at Heydon and Beeston next Mileham, Norfolk.

Always look at the end walls of the nave for signs of the former nave roof. These are most likely to be seen on the eastern face of the west tower (11). Sometimes the traces of three or more roof levels may be seen, as at Burford, on the west side of the central tower.

These roof marks will often indicate by their level whether the arcade has since been raised, or whether the nave possessed a clerestory of older date than that now existing; also whether the clerestory is earlier or later in date than the tower. The absence of any roof marks against the tower is good evidence that the tower is later.

In cases where an early nave has been widened in later times, the shape of the older nave is sometimes clearly outlined on the east wall, as at Tostock.

In assigning an exact date to the original construction of the aisles it should be borne in mind that the earlier aisles were always very narrow, and covered in many cases by a continuation of the roof of the nave (12).

Really wide aisles did not come into general use before the middle of the thirteenth century. After that time aisles were often widened or heightened, or both, so it is worth while to examine the end walls to see whether there are any marks of the earlier aisle remaining. Sometimes the width and the pitch of the roof are plainly seen, usually at the west end, as at Charlbury, Oxfordshire; Hallaton, Leicestershire; or Chiddingfold, Surrey. In cases of heightening only, there will not only be some trace of the earlier pitch, but also a difference in the masonry of the upper part of the side wall, as at Cockfield, Suffolk. A comparison of the two aisles is often useful, as one of them may retain its original proportions. It is far safer to date the aisle by its base course and its buttresses than by its side windows, which are very likely to be later insertions. The east and west windows of an aisle are most likely to be the original ones, and in some cases where the west window seems very low set and out of the centre it will be found that it is a relic of an earlier and narrower aisle.

Very exceptionally a nave was widened by removing an arcade and absorbing an aisle. This happened at Rainham, Kent, and Mapledurham, Oxfordshire.

Transeptal chapels are usually later developments, and unless they are obviously pre-Conquest as at Worth, Sussex, they are likely to be of the thirteenth century or later (14).

A cruciform church, that is, one possessing a central tower (9, 44, 78, 96) and transepts, or one showing signs that it was once cruciform, is likely to be of fairly early foundation, and certainly not later than the thirteenth century, however late the work above ground may be. Signs of the former possession of a central tower are the wider span of the eastern arch of the nave arcades, or a thickening of the walls towards the eastern part of the nave. Sometimes the responds of the former tower arches remain, as at Tamworth, Staffordshire.

It is important to note whether the side arches of the central tower (15) are of the same date as those to east and west. If of different dates it is reasonable to suppose that the church was originally without transepts. Obviously the style of the arches fixes the date of the first building of the transepts, however much these latter may have been rebuilt in later times. The eastern walls of transepts should always be inspected in hopes of finding traces of arches opening into eastern chapels now vanished.

As in the nave, the aisles or clerestories are generally later improvements to transepts, but not invariably so.

In the chancel the first portion to be investigated is the western section of the side walls. Note any break in the courses of the masonry, in the base course or string courses within and without, which may indicate a later eastward extension. The east window is very likely to be a later insertion, and the best way of ascertaining the date of the east wall, whether original or an enlargement, is the base course and the buttresses. If the sill level does not agree with the level of the string course it is safe to assume that the east wall is earlier than its window. Traces of earlier windows in a blocked condition often remain on either side of an east window, or below its sill.

If the chancel seems very lofty or spacious, the wall above the chancel arch will sometimes give an indication of its former size, either by the survival of the marks of the roof, or by a change in the masonry.

Chancel aisles may be of any post-Conquest date, but generally they are additions and are likely to be later than the middle of the thirteenth century. They are practically always later than nave aisles.

BAY DESIGN.—The stone vault made a regular division into bays absolutely essential in the great churches from the twelfth century on, but as the parish churches were rarely intended for a stone vault and the types of roof construction known were of the single-framed variety—exercising a uniform thrust all along the wall, with no members dropping below the wall-plate—there was no necessity for exact correspondence between arch and window and pier and buttress. It is only in the rare vaulted buildings that one finds a definite system until the fourteenth century, and it is not until the very end of that century that one finds exact and systematic correspondence between buttresses and piers. Such regularity is rarely found except in East Anglia, where the early development of the timber roof on scientific and decorative lines made it essential.

PORCHES are generally one of the latest additions to the ground plan of a church, and almost all examples are later than the end of the twelfth century. Porches exist in several places with Norman outer doorways, but it will generally be found that the porch itself is later and that the original doorway of the nave has been utilised in the new building, as at Foresthill, Oxfordshire. Thirteenth-century porches are not common, and it was not until the fifteenth century that they were regarded as a necessity.

When a porch was built on to an aisleless nave it often prevented the addition of a later aisle, or confined the aisle to the eastern bays of the nave, a state of things very common in Dorset and South Somerset. A porch added to a narrow aisle has often prevented the widening so common in the fourteenth century and later, as at Witney, Bishop's Cleeve (9) or Shifnal, or only the eastern portion has been widened, while in one or two cases the widening has been carried out at the expense of the porch, as at West Walton (82).

When a porch is contemporary with the aisle (or with the nave if the church is aisleless), one would expect to find a continuity in the base course, but this is seldom found.

Porches have rarely been altered in plan, but the addition of an upper stage is by no means uncommon.

TOWERS are very often the only surviving relic of the earlier structure, and more pre-Conquest towers (21, 27, 28) have survived than naves or chancels, for the reconstruction of a tower was a serious matter, not to be lightly undertaken. On the other hand, very many churches

13

were originally built without towers (20, 34). If the tower is western, it is interesting to note whether it is bonded to the nave or not. Some were built against the west wall of the nave, and may hide an older west façade, as at Brixworth, Much Wenlock or Saxthorpe. More often the whole of the west wall was taken down, but it was convenient to build the tower just beyond the nave and to link up the new work afterwards, slightly lengthening the nave ; and when this has been done the result is easily apparent. Many western towers were built inside the west end of the nave, as at Water Eaton or Northmoor in Oxfordshire. Much less often a later axial tower has been inserted at the east end of the nave, as at Willersey, Brimpsfield or Hempstead.

In some churches a central tower has fallen or, having shown signs of falling, has been taken down, and a new tower has been built at the west end. Tamworth and High Wycombe are obvious instances of this. More rarely a tower at the side of the nave has been abandoned and a western tower erected, as at Great Yeldham and perhaps at Much Wenlock.

It is safe to say that a tower is likely to be either much earlier or much later than the main building period, since then, as now, there was a limit to the amount of work that could be undertaken at one time. For instance, the churches of Blythburgh, St. Mary's, Oxford, Ewelme and Shelton were completely rebuilt in the later Gothic period, with the exception of the tower. Most towers in this country are of the fifteenth century or later.

Many towers have been heightened in later times (17), and some show as many as three or four different styles in the successive stages. If a tower has more than three stages it is likely that the fourth was an afterthought, except in Somerset, where four stages are the rule in the finer towers. It is not always safe to say that the upper stages are later than the lower. There are many exceptions, strange as it may seem. Many central towers stand on arches inserted at a later date, for instance Norton, Co. Durham, and Cholsey, and rare instances are known where the spire is of earlier date than the tower which supports it.

DOORWAYS.—The re-use of old materials will sometimes explain otherwise insoluble problems, but the theory should always be adopted with great caution. Norman doorways, owing to their great charm, were very often utilised in later work. It is by no means uncommon to find certain proof that the doorway, originally in the side wall of an early nave, has been utilised in a narrow thirteenth-century aisle, and has again been inserted in a still later widening of the same aisle. Norman doorways were often re-used in later porches, as at Castle Ashby and Askham Bryan, and at Morwenstow it seems as if some of the superfluous rings of voussoirs of an exceptionally elaborate doorway were used as the outer doorway of a porch which still protects the remainder.

There are also many churches where, on the addition of an aisle to the chancel, the windows from the latter, displaced by the arcade, were used

11 MOULTON, LINCOLNSHIRE, FROM THE SOUTH-EAST. Geometrical South Aisle, Early Perpendicular Tower and Spire

10 THE SPACIOUS PERPENDICULAR NAVE OF BLAKENEY, NORFOLK

12 BURY, SUSSEX: Early English with shingled broach Spire

in the new construction, as at Crewkerne ; or the east window of the nave aisle has been utilised in a later chancel aisle, as at Castleacre or Chipping Campden. Sedilia and piscinæ were often re-used in new positions. But such re-use of old material is not common, and imitation of older work is extremely rare and is never a safe theory to rely upon.

*   *   *   *   *   *   *

To get the full enjoyment from an old church it is very important not to let oneself become obsessed with the idea of antiquity. Some beginners are so impressed with the age of a building that they seem to imagine that its builders were doddering greybeards. Now mediæval architecture is really full of the spirit of youth. The Gothic craftsmen were much more alive than we are, with a lively sense of humour. Old men were scarce in the Middle Ages, for life was much more precarious and cheaper than nowadays, so we shall not be far wrong in saying that our ancient churches were built by young men.

Do not fall into the mistake of thinking that the artistic value or beauty of a building is in direct ratio to its age, or despise the later work simply because it is not so old. Above all, do not take on trust the opinions of old-fashioned archæologists as to the merits of this or that style. It used to be held that Gothic art grew to perfection and then gradually declined. The period of highest achievement was reached, according to some, in the middle of the fourteenth century, or about 1300 or 1260, or even in the Transitional period of the late twelfth century, according to the personal preferences of the writer concerned. The view that Gothic architecture reached perfection very soon and declined gradually for some three hundred years, until it was put out of its misery, as it were, by the Renaissance of the sixteenth century, is fast losing ground. Parish church architecture, at least, continued to advance after 1260, and most of our finest buildings are mainly of later date (10, 140, 145). What is lost in the freshness and charm of the unsophisticated and experimental early work (4, 67, 87) is gained in the finer feeling for proportion and beauty of detail, the greater height and scale (5, 6, 111), and the more competent and systematic planning. It is an indisputable fact that the average parish church of the fifteenth century (145) was far more convenient, more spacious, better lighted and more graceful, and was better fitted for its purpose, than a building of similar rank of the twelfth (34) or thirteenth (74) centuries.

Every period has its own particular appeal, and every one has a right to his own particular preference. At the same time, it ought to be recognised that, from the millennium onwards, generation after generation of builders were continuously striving to achieve this ideal of the spacious, well-lighted church, in which every stone was essential and related to the rest of the building, an ideal which was only fully realised in such late work as Long Melford, St. Mary's Nottingham, Lavenham (145), Hull (111), Tickhill (19), St. Neot's Huntingdonshire (18), or Blakeney (10), and many others of equally late date.

15

CHAPTER III

BEGINNINGS OF THE SAXON STYLE

CHRISTIANITY itself was for a time overwhelmed in the invasions of North European tribes during the fifth and sixth centuries, only to rise again and conquer the conquerors. Now these invading tribes, whether Angles, Saxons or Jutes, knew nothing of building in stone. They were farmers, shipbuilders, and invaders from necessity rather than from choice, owing to the pressure of the great westward movement of the peoples of Europe.

They had to learn the art of building from its very beginning. What they built after their conversion was in imitation of the ruins of Romano-British buildings. That this is a fact we may gather from Bede, whose greatest praise for a church is that it was built in the Roman manner. They would have been incapable of re-inventing the arch. That they copied from Roman buildings, and the fact that the joints of their arches seldom radiate correctly, shows how little they understood its principles. Again, from classic sources they derived their love of large stones in quoins and jambs (20). They might not have thought of the circular column (31) if they had not had Roman examples before their eyes. In effect, they had to start and learn to build; so the story of English church architecture is the story of the art of building from its beginnings to its perfection.

ROMANO-BRITISH SOURCES.—Though the first Saxon or Anglian church builders knew less of architecture than the most ignorant amateur of to-day, they had the advantage of starting with but one preconceived idea, and that a sound one, namely that the old Roman manner of building was admirable and to be followed as closely as possible.

What were the characteristics of the provincial Roman architecture? If we conjure up visions of stately colonnaded buildings and vast halls we shall certainly go astray. It was a very simple style, practical rather than ornamental, carried out in the local material, with much use of large thin bricks where freestone was not obtainable; some walls were entirely faced with brick. The openings were small and spanned either by lintels of wood or stone, or by arches in stone or brick. Cornices and entablatures, columns and pediments were only employed in very important buildings, and their proportions were only vaguely reminiscent of the classic orders of Imperial Rome.

For the most part it was utilitarian building, reduced to its simplest expression. The flat roofs and obtuse pediments suitable to Italy were

14 THE EAST SIDE OF THE SOUTH TRANSEPT
WITH UNUSUAL CHAPEL AND PORCH

UFFINGTON, BERKSHIRE: CRUCIFORM EARLY ENGLISH

13 THE CHANCEL, EAST END
The cruciform panels contain consecration crosses

15 BROADWATER, SUSSEX : the crossing from the west

16 CHEPSTOW, MONMOUTHSHIRE : the West Front

NORMAN ARCH DESIGN

abandoned in northern climes, and roofs were generally high-pitched to suit the local roofing materials. None survive, but the roofing and ridge tiles and stone slates found on Roman sites prove conclusively that their angle was fairly acute. Where flint or small stone rubble was the local material, openings and quoins were formed in Roman brick and the same material was freely used in horizontal bands to bind the wall longitudinally. Where the local material was a freestone, this was squared more or less roughly with the axe into convenient blocks for facing, usually not very large, but very big stones were often used for quoins of the jambs of openings or for lintels.

The provincial Roman style was one which could easily be carried out by partly skilled or by unskilled labour; much of it was the work of the military. There is little carving, and that for the most part mere amateur effort, based on a recollection of classic technique but without any definite craft tradition behind it.

Such were the buildings which remained as models for the Saxon church builder, but in addition he knew of the existence of finer buildings in other lands, and even in Rome itself, from the accounts of pilgrims and his ecclesiastical employers, who were in fairly close touch with Rome and demanded buildings which should resemble those they had seen and admired.

ROMAN SOURCES.—Were any churches built in Britain during the Roman occupation and do any remains exist? Modern excavations have thrown much light on the Romano-British civilisation, but the evidence on this point is slight. At Silchester were unearthed the foundations of a tiny building with a western apse, transepts and aisles on both sides, and a porch or narthex across the east end. The plan agrees so exactly with that of the normal Christian church in the Roman provinces that it may be regarded as practically certain that the building is a church. Likewise, at Caerleon, a small apsidal-ended structure may be another church. Some antiquaries have maintained that portions of the churches of St. Martin's at Canterbury and Reculver, Kent, are actually of Roman building, and the material of these is certainly Roman, but that is no proof of the date of the walls, for the re-use of Roman masonry and brickwork and the imitation of Roman methods of building is a commonplace of later Saxon building. Reculver can be dismissed at once, but St. Martin's has a stronger claim, since we have documentary evidence that a Romano-British church stood on the site. The portions of this undoubtedly very ancient church which claim to be actually of Roman date are the western portions of the side walls of the chancel. A large nave built at the west end has encroached on the west end of the older structure, and its eastern façade, which appears, from foundations discovered some years ago, to have had a small apse, obviously not original, was destroyed when the chancel was extended in the thirteenth century. No foundations have been discovered at the west end; but the building certainly extended some distance farther westward. The walls are almost entirely faced with Roman brick. It seems to be not unlikely that here we have the remains of a small Romano-British church of perhaps the fourth century, and the most likely explanation of the somewhat fragmentary plan is that the original church faced west and terminated in the usual apse at that end, somewhere in the middle of the present nave. At the same time, it must be remembered that experts say the masonry is too clumsy to be of Roman date, and the only argument which can be brought against them is that the church of a small sect might well be less carefully built than the official structures of a great empire. If St. Martin's is not Roman, we must say that no Romano-British church exists above the surface of the ground.

CELTIC SOURCES.—But some of the characteristics of our earliest churches are derived from another source. Not all of England, and still less of Wales, had been brought under Roman control, yet Christianity had penetrated at an early date, and by channels now forgotten, as far as Ireland and the Western Isles. In Cornwall, West Devon, Mid-Wales, and, generally speaking, in all the Celtic as opposed to Anglo-Saxon districts, no trace can be seen of any Roman tradition in the earliest churches. The oldest are not churches as we now understand the word; halls to accommodate the altar, the clergy serving it, and the worshippers, all under one roof. They were mere shrines to protect the altar, and the worshippers stood without. They were built according to the local native method, by the missionary and his converts, none of whom had any knowledge of classic tradition. Some of the oldest were beehive huts, stone versions of the ice igloos of the Esquimaux of to-day, of circular plan, roofed by gradually projecting each course of blocks inwards until they met. Rather later the rectangular plan was adopted and roofed in the same manner by corbelling over the side walls. Of decoration there was none. There was always a small door at the west end, framed by upright blocks, usually of large size, which leaned towards one another to reduce the span of the lintel, and there was sometimes a small square-headed window at the east end, where the altar stood. The method of building was a survival of the Stone Age, apart from and independent of the main stream of architectural tradition and based on common sense and necessity alone.

Not all these little churches or oratories were of stone. Bede says quite clearly that the manner of the Scots, i.e., Celts, was to build in wood and not in stone. Many, perhaps most, of the oratories of the Celtic missionaries must have been little log-huts built of upright trunks of trees, a method which can still be seen in a building of much later date, the church of Greenstead, Essex. Others may have been of wattle and daub, like that which Joseph of Arimathea is reputed to have built at Glastonbury.

One thing is quite certain, that in the early Celtic Church the worshippers stood in the open air about a little shrine, as did their pagan forefathers,

17 A GREAT MARSHLAND CHURCH, GEDNEY, LINCOLNSHIRE. Largely Perpendicular, Tower Early English, with Perpendicular heightening and Decorated work to the west of the South Aisle

18 ST. NEOT'S, HUNTINGDONSHIRE

PERPENDICULAR DESIGN

19 TICKHILL, YORKSHIRE

not to mention the ancient Greeks and the Israelites of old, a practice entirely different from that of the Christians of the Roman Empire, whose idea of a church was a great hall in which the congregation could assemble.

It also seems certain that the pagan Saxons were not accustomed to worshipping inside a building. Their rites were carried out in sacred enclosures, marked by wood fences, stone circles, or earthworks, and they undoubtedly took over the sacred places of the former inhabitants, just as the Turks turned churches into mosques or the French revolutionaries made churches serve as Temples of Liberty.

Their conversion was effected by missionaries, Celtic and Roman— the one attack from the North and West bringing the tradition of worship in the open air about a little shrine, the other, from the South-east, introducing the practice of assembling in a hall.

St. Augustine's Mission.—We have all read in our history books of St. Gregory sending St. Augustine to convert the Angles into angels, but have probably forgotten the date, 597. He found that Christianity had arrived before him. The King of Kent, Ethelbert, had married a Christian Frankish princess who was in the habit even then of worshipping in a church dedicated to St. Martin, in Canterbury, built in the days of the Roman occupation. There is still a church of St. Martin, one of the oldest in England, and, as we have seen, it is just possible that the western part of the chancel is actually a fragment of the church in which Bertha, Queen of Kent, worshipped.

Bede tells us that Ethelbert was converted and allowed the missionaries to build and repair churches in all places. Fragments or foundations of several of the churches built by St. Augustine and his immediate successors still exist, and one, built not more than sixty years after his death, still has a roof. These are the churches of St. Peter and St. Paul, St. Pancras and St. Mary at Canterbury, the foundations of another at Lyminge, the remains of a large church at Reculver, and the complete nave of St. Peter's, Bradwell-on-Sea, Essex. They are all much of a type, and were all built between 597 and 666. Their plan is a nave and apsidal chancel, separated by a triple chancel arch. The walls, like those of the early Christian buildings of Italy, are thin. The nave and chancel are of the same width. Three of these, St. Peter and Paul at Canterbury, Lyminge and Reculver were monastic churches, but they do not differ essentially from the purely parochial churches of St. Pancras, St. Mary or Bradwell-on-Sea. Several have chambers attached at the side, apparently chapels, but not open to the nave. At St. Peter and St. Paul they occupy the whole length of the nave and the narthex, which appears in this example only. At St. Pancras they are some distance from the chancel. At St. Peter's, Bradwell-on-Sea, and at Reculver they overlap the chancel. A western porch, possibly a later addition, is a feature of the plans of St. Pancras and Bradwell.

So far as can be judged by the remaining fragments, their architectural style is provincial Roman. The doorways seem to have been plain, with semicircular heads cut straight through the wall. The windows at Reculver seem to have been similar, but narrow, but those at Bradwell-on-Sea were wide and slightly splayed, that at the west end with a semicircular arch, those at the side with wood lintels. The triple chancel arch of Reculver stood till the early nineteenth century, when it was destroyed, but the columns which supported it are now at Canterbury. They are of classic proportions and the shafts may be re-used Roman work, but the capitals and bases are only crude imitations of Roman technique. The triple arcade at Bradwell-on-Sea can still be traced in the blocked east wall. At St. Pancras one of the bases remains and seems to be a Roman attic base re-used. The proportions of these arcades are reminiscent of those which separate the aisles from the naves of the basilicas of Italy.

Though several of these churches had side chapels built on, none were aisled, though Reculver seems to have added aisles at a rather later date. Most modern writers seem to limit the word basilica to those churches which possess aisles. I do not think it was so limited by Bede and the other chroniclers of early Church history. Bede when he records the building of a basilica does not necessarily mean an aisled building but a church housing both altar and worshippers, as opposed to the Celtic oratory or cell, which was intended only to shelter the altar.

The plan of this group of churches is peculiar, and has little in common with the early churches of Italy. The only precedent for the triple chancel arch in Italy is the doubtful example, cited by Rivoira, of the so-called church of St. Cesarion-al-Palatino. Aisleless churches are unknown in Italy, even the tiniest having arcaded naves. Nor can the aisleless plan be derived from Romano-British sources, since the only certain example, Silchester, though exceedingly small, is aisled.

Another peculiarity of these churches is that they have the apse at the east end. The earliest churches of Rome, and Silchester also, have western apses, and the entrance at the east like the Tabernacle in the wilderness. But before the time of Augustine churches with eastern orientation had been built at Ravenna. It seems likely that the change of direction was due to pre-Christian pagan influences, not unconnected with the worship of the sun, particularly as St. Gregory counselled Augustine to deal gently with heathen practices when they were not directly opposed to Christianity. Certain it is that henceforward all English churches were built with the altar at the east end.

There are two more early churches very little later than the group we have been considering, the large and remarkably well-preserved church, once monastic, at Brixworth (26), and the remains of a much smaller one at Lydd, now incorporated into a large mediæval structure. Both of these had aisles and seem to have had the triple chancel arch, showing the influence of the early Kentish group, and both are built with Roman material and somewhat in the Roman manner. Brixworth had also a single arch opening into the apse and still retains its clerestory (26), the earliest now existing in England, though it has lost its aisles. It has also a crypt under the chancel, an indication of strong Italian influence. It is a decidedly impressive building on a very large scale, and the effect of the Roman brick combined with local ironstone is very striking, though it was undoubtedly plastered externally in the first place.

In both these buildings the arcades have arches of small span and huge rectangular piers, showing nothing of the influence of the graceful arcades of Roman or Ravennate churches.

The latest example which can be derived from St. Augustine's churches is the very interesting aisled church at Wing (23), with its polygonal apse, having a crypt below. Though there are sundry late details it seems to have more affinity with Brixworth than with any later building.

THE CELTIC GROUP OF EARLY CHURCHES. — Meanwhile Celtic missionaries had been penetrating for years from the North, building little oratories of stone, and when the Celtic and Roman traditions met, as they did in Northumberland and Durham, the result was a compromise, as usual with Englishmen of all ages. Benedict Biscop, Abbot of Wearmouth and Jarrow, had been to Rome and wished to introduce Roman customs. Particularly he wanted to build stone churches in the Roman manner. Bede tells us that he introduced foreign workmen for the purpose from Gaul, but this statement must be taken with caution. We have always attributed anything of unusual architectural beauty to foreigners, and there is nothing in the buildings which he caused to be put up to remind us of Gaul or Italy. The solution which his craftsmen applied to the problem of building basilicas in the Roman manner was to splice on to a cell of the usual Celtic type a nave of similar proportions but much larger dimensions to shelter the congregation. At Monkwearmouth only the nave is left. At Jarrow only the chancel, but at Escomb (20), a little contemporary village church, both nave and chancel remain, giving a good idea of the former appearance of the two larger churches. Bede calls them both basilicas, but anything less like a Roman basilica it would be difficult to imagine. The proportions are altogether different from even the Kentish group ; the naves are longer and narrower and probably much more lofty, the chancels narrower still, and much lower than the nave. In place of the great triumphal arch of the Roman churches, or the lofty triple arcade of the Kentish group, there is one very narrow arch, almost shutting off the chancel, and much more reminiscent of the west doorway of a Celtic oratory. Instead of a stately apse the cramped chancel is square-ended.

These buildings were newly built from the foundations, but it is very likely indeed that in some cases the same result was reached by adding a larger building to the west of an existing cell. The plan was a compromise, but it met with much more success than the more perfect Kentish plan.

It was generally adopted in Northumbria and spread all over Saxon England, and was in fact the normal plan for a small parish church all through the Middle Ages.

One fact that may be adduced in support of this theory of its origin is that to this day the parishioners are responsible for the upkeep of the nave, while the rector must keep the chancel in repair. Possibly this is a relic of the days when the missioner built his little cell, perhaps with his own hands, and carried on until sufficient converts had been made and sufficient enthusiasm raised for the building of a nave. The plan has great defects, for it is unfit that the altar should be housed in a portion of the building lower and narrower than the other part of the church.

There is a feature found in both these groups of early churches, which is only indirectly derived from Roman sources, namely, the west porch. The typical Roman church had a sort of porch stretching right across the façade, termed the narthex. In this country it appears in the Romano-British church at Silchester and in St. Augustine's church of St. Peter and St. Paul at Canterbury. But at St. Pancras, Canterbury and Bradwell-on-Sea, in the southern group, and at Monkwearmouth and Corbridge in the North, a small west porch takes its place. It was evidently a cheap substitute for the narthex. But the interesting point is that later, probably when the first Viking raids were making some sort of look-out a necessity, several of these west porches were heightened and turned into west towers. This position for a tower is unknown in Italy, and indeed in all southern lands, and is peculiar to North-west Europe. All through the Middle Ages the middle of the west front was the favourite position for the tower, and its origin may be traced to these western porches.

The nave and chancel plan did not reach Cornwall or Mid-Wales at all, and only penetrated into Devon, the Welsh seaboard and the Lake district after the Norman Conquest. The source of the Christianity of these districts was wholly Celtic; direct Roman influence was negligible. The cell developed into a little church quite naturally, by building larger and larger cells. The tradition was so strong that, though the Normans built nave and chancel churches in Devon, at least, these were generally changed to the traditional local plan in the fifteenth century.

In 731 Bede closes his history with a glowing account of the state of the Church at that time, the state of peace, the triumph of Christianity. The only crumpled rose leaf was the fact that the Britons, the inhabitants of the western fringes of England, were still obstinate in refusing to celebrate Easter at the time prescribed by the Roman Church. " What the end will be," says Bede, " the next age will show." And the next age was a series of suicidal struggles between the kingdoms in England, followed by the murderous raids of the Danes. There were periods of quiet, and there are records of many important churches being built in the two centuries following the conclusion of Bede's history, but it is impossible to refer

20 ESCOMB, CO. DURHAM

21 KIRK HAMMERTON, YORKSHIRE

SAXON VILLAGE CHURCHES

23   THE SAXON APSE AND CRYPT, WING,
BUCKINGHAMSHIRE

22   THE SAXON TOWER, BARTON-ON-HUMBER,
LINCOLNSHIRE

the remains of any existing churches to this period. All that is practically certain is that during this epoch the cruciform plan was evolved.

At the end of the seventh century St. Wilfrid had caused to be built at Hexham a round church having four chapels about it; obviously after a Roman model, for Rome had circular as well as rectangular churches from the first days of Christian liberty. Now a circular church is a difficult thing to build, and still more difficult to roof. It seems to call for a dome, which needs great engineering skill. If the church is a square on plan it is far easier to build. That was the plan adopted at Athelney in the church of the monastery founded by Alfred the Great at the end of the ninth century, judging from the description of William of Malmesbury, a great square tower with four gabled limbs projecting from it.

Just as the seventh-century builders of the North built their churches very narrow and obtained a certain degree of dignity by making them of lofty proportions, we may be certain that the central space of Athelney, the crossing, was of no great span and that it was carried up in the form of a tower, as in several early buildings in France. The plan never fell into disuse, but in the course of time the central space was reduced in width and the arms of the cross widened until they were equal to that of the crossing. The western limb especially needed to be larger than the others, since it served as a nave. The main advantage of widening the side arms or transepts was that so they afforded better abutment to the arches of the crossing, which was sorely needed when it was carried up as a tower, and this was usually done so that windows could be formed above the roofs of the four limbs of the cross. Most of our early towers were lantern towers for the purpose of lighting the crossing.

CHAPTER IV

THE LATER PRE-CONQUEST STYLE

An era more favourable to the growth of architecture set in with the reign of Edgar (959-975). Practically all our existing pre-Conquest building seems to belong to the century between this era of peace and the Norman Conquest. There is a tendency on the part of most modern writers to assign the majority of examples to the reign of Edward the Confessor in the middle of the eleventh century, but it seems likely that, as knowledge increases, it will be possible to assign to many examples a much earlier date—to the period of St. Dunstan's influence, or to the reign of Canute.

This later pre-Conquest architecture has a distinct character of its own. It is, as we have seen, derived from Roman and Celtic sources and attempts to combine the two traditions. But it is also an architecture of experiment, and to the trials and errors of the pre-Conquest masons we owe the more systematic Norman style.

The Celtic builders had no system of ornament applied to building. The Romans regarded decoration as something altogether apart from construction. It was the tenth and eleventh century builders who gradually developed a system of decorating the essential parts of the structure, and evolved that characteristic feature of mediæval architecture, the arch constructed in several overhanging rings of small stones.

The percentage of our churches which retain pre-Conquest work is small, but collectively they afford a sufficient body of evidence to enable us to form a clear idea of the main characteristics of the period. The very scarcity of examples makes pre-Conquest work a fascinating branch of study. Practically every English county can show one or two examples, and in some counties—Gloucester, Hampshire, Sussex, Essex for instance—the number of pre-Conquest churches runs into two figures. Very often the remains are so embedded in later work that they escape notice completely. The list of examples is constantly being lengthened as our churches are more completely and thoroughly surveyed.

None of our pre-Conquest buildings, with the possible exception of the tower of Earls Barton (27), achieves any high degree of beauty or dignity, but it is impossible to resist the attraction of these simple and artless efforts to produce a manner of building which should meet the needs and conditions of the time—efforts which we know finally resulted in the triumphs of fourteenth and fifteenth century building.

PLANNING.—We have seen how the Celtic tradition of small oratories meeting with the Roman tradition of large halls resulted in the two-chambered nave and chancel plan which was to be the normal type of parish church all through the Middle Ages ; how in the West the small rectangular oratory swelled into a larger rectangle ; how Wilfrid attempted to introduce the circular plan with radiating chapels, from Italy, in the seventh century, and how this was squared at Athelney, resulting in the cruciform church with a central tower.

The single-chamber plan undoubtedly prevailed in the West all through the Anglo-Saxon period, but owing to the extreme simplicity of the architecture, the absence of freestone and the entire lack of datable features, it is difficult to cite certain examples. Yet many of the churches of Mid and North Wales are quite as likely to be of the eighth or ninth century as of the twelfth, for there was no great period of rebuilding in Wales in the twelfth century as in England.

Such churches as Llanrychwy and the nave of Eglwys Cwm in Cardiganshire are quite likely to be pre-Conquest, especially as the latter has the typical wide stone roof. A similar building, quite likely to be of very early date, is the chapel on Tor Hill at Torquay, with its rugged walls and crude solid stone roof. The remains of similar rectangular buildings, perhaps of pre-Conquest date, exist in Cornwall at Perranzabuloe, St. Gwithian and Madron. One cannot dogmatise as to their actual date, but it can at least be definitely stated that, in the absence of any evidence of nave and chancel plans, still less of cruciform plans, they represent the most ancient tradition of the West.

The nave and chancel plan is by far the commonest in pre-Conquest building from the seventh century onwards. Examples are very numerous. Usually the nave is longer, narrower and much more lofty than that of a post-Conquest building, and the chancel is also very narrow, lofty, and extremely short (20, 21).

Transeptal chapels were often added to the nave, following the primitive method of adding porches for chapels. Worth has two, slightly later in date than the nave fabric. Britford, rather earlier, has the two arches which formerly led to transeptal chapels, and the triangular arch on the north side of Bicester is possibly another example.

Western porches were a feature of seventh and eighth century churches, and were afterwards carried up as west towers, as at Corbridge, Monkwearmouth and Brixworth ; and in later churches a lofty and slender tower was very often built in this position (28).

The cruciform plan with central tower was probably never very common, and examples range over a period of 150 years at least. Breamore is probably late tenth century, Wootton Wawen is but little later. Repton (31) is almost certainly tenth century, Dover of very uncertain date, perhaps c. 1000, while Stow and Great Paxton are probably of the time of the Confessor.

D   25

Some of the churches with central towers never had transepts. One of the earliest of these is Barton-on-Humber (22), where the western limb survives and the eastern limb, though destroyed, is known to have existed. Bracebridge, Lincolnshire, seems not to have had a western limb. Later examples of churches with central towers but no transepts are North Leigh, Newton, Langford and Great Dunham.

Aisles were rarely employed before the Conquest. Wilfrid's churches at Hexham and Ripon certainly had aisles, and so had many of the Saxon cathedrals. St. Augustine's churches were without aisles, but they were subsequently added at Reculver. Brixworth (2, 26) is the oldest existing example of an aisled church, and our other fragment, slightly later in date, is the remains of a tiny aisled church at Lydd. Wing (23) is a late survival of the Brixworth plan. Repton is stated to have had aisles. Of the latest period, the only surviving examples seem to be Great Paxton and Ickleton.

The entrance was generally from the west, and side porches are uncommon. They occur at Bradford-on-Avon and Bishopstone, where they are large, with the doorway out of the centre, towards the west, suggesting that they contained altars and were used as chapels.

The chancel was generally square-ended. St. Augustine's churches had apses—so have Brixworth and Wing (23). The foundations of the apses of Deerhurst exist, and Worth still retains its eastern round, much restored ; but against these few examples there are some three dozen existing examples of the square end.

Aisles to the chancel are unknown, but there may be flanking chambers as at Brixworth and Wing.

WALLS.—The methods employed by the builders of the later pre-Conquest period offer a good many peculiarities. Their love of big stones was remarkable. The walls are generally very thin, frequently no more than 2 ft. or 2 ft. 3 in., and any so-called pre-Conquest work having walls above 2 ft. 6 in. in thickness should be looked upon with suspicion. Generally they are a good deal more carefully bonded and the mortar is of better quality than in Norman work. When Roman and British material was available it was still very freely used. In stoneless districts Roman bricks were very commonly employed and even lumps of masonry, still bound together with the old mortar, were sometimes pressed into service. In freestone districts Roman ashlars, quoins, and archways or monolith shafts were ruthlessly stolen from the old ruins and utilised.

Very large stones were much sought after for quoins and dressings. These were used in two distinct ways. Probably the earliest method was to lay great oblong blocks, and these continued to be used after the second method was introduced. This is the famous long and short work, an infallible indication of fairly late pre-Conquest date. It would be better described as slab and block. The normal method of quoining (20, 21)

24 and 25 SAXON WINDOWS, BARNACK, NORTHAMPTONSHIRE

26 THE SOUTH SIDE, BRIXWORTH, NORTHAMPTONSHIRE

28 FORNCETT ST. PETER, NORFOLK

27 EARL'S BARTON, NORTHAMPTONSHIRE

SAXON TOWERS

shows a short stone on one face and a long one on the other, while the " long and short " quoin (27) shows a short on both faces, and the next stone shows long on both faces. Sometimes the blocks are very tall in proportion to their width.

In flint districts quoins were sometimes formed with great difficulty in large flints, but Roman bricks were preferred if they were to be had.

Base courses do not occur in the earlier work, but in later building there are sometimes a few projecting courses at the base of the wall, not, as a rule, weathered or chamfered on the top edge.

The stages of the building were sometimes marked by fairly shallow projecting courses of ashlar, corresponding to the later storey courses, but they were almost invariably square-edged and of very slight projection. Though sometimes of considerable depth, they divide the stages of towers of such widely differing dates as Monkwearmouth and Earls Barton, and are used beneath the window sills at Worth or beneath the wall arcades of Bradford-on-Avon.

Narrow projecting vertical strips of wrought stone, called pilaster strips (22, 27), were very commonly used where freestone was the local material, and even where none could be had the same effect was obtained in large flints or pebbles covered with plaster. They are purely decorative, and seem to be a relic of the classic use of pilasters to make the bay division of a building, but at this period they had no such excuse and are more erratically spaced. They are usually very narrow and of slight projection. Sometimes they occur on the angle of a building, worked on the quoin stones. One or two buildings which authorities regard as fairly early examples have diagonal pilasters (22, 27), giving the effect of a seventeenth-century half-timber building petrified. It is not safe to dogmatise, but so far as our knowledge has reached, pilaster strips seem to be a mark of fairly early Saxon work of the latest period. It is likely that this very characteristic feature was more used *c.* 1000 than *c.* 1060.

A frieze of wall-arcading of a primitive kind in rubble, with triangular heads, occurs at Geddington, and is probably contemporary with Earls Barton. Shallow wall-arcading occurs in the beautifully built chapel at Bradford-on-Avon, probably early eleventh century, where the arches are sunk in the masonry of the wall. An interior wall-arcade in flint covered with plaster occurs at Great Dunham.

Often a fragment of pilaster work remains over the nave arcade towards the aisle of a building altered in post-Conquest times, as at Bibury.

All wrought stonework of this date is exceedingly irregular and erratic. The angles of the blocks are only approximately right angles. Symmetrical features rarely balance. It is as if all the work were done freehand without the aid of the square.

ARCHES.—The Saxons knew three distinct ways of bridging over an opening. The lintel, used both in Romano-British and in Celtic buildings, they sometimes employed, and very often the under side of the lintel was cut into the shape of an arch. The semicircular arch they borrowed from Romano-British building. The third method, inclined stones propped up against each other forming a sort of triangular arch (25, 30), they probably got from Irish sources. They even did the same thing in Roman brick if large stones could not be obtained, as at Holy Trinity, Colchester.

Most pre-Conquest arches differ from those of a later date because, following Roman practice, the arch stones, or most of them, are of the full thickness of the wall, running through from back to front. There are one or two cases of the long and short principle being applied to an arch, as at Britford, the arch stones being alternately two small ones with a space between, filled in with brick or rubble, and one long thin stone, but that is unusual ; in nine cases out of ten the stones run right through the wall. This was done partly because of the primitive delight in large stones, and partly to economise centering. Only two arch ribs were necessary and those did not have to be boarded over.

In a few late examples the arches are in two rings, but both rings run right through the wall and the faces of both are flush with it. Often a sort of projecting pilaster strip is bent round the upper surface of the arch to give a finished effect—the germ of the hood mould (22, 32, 33).

SUPPORTS.—The classic tradition of the Orders was practically dead, but still the craftsmen felt that a cylindrical column was fittest, that something was necessary to give a spread to the base and to adapt the circular shaft to the square arch above it. Some attempt to imitate classic moulded bases was sometimes made, but this was very half-hearted and indefinite. A square base block sometimes sufficed, or a sort of caricature of classic moulding, but there was never any sort of accepted formula for base moulds.

Capitals were equally sketchy ; a sort of cushion cap was sometimes employed, relieved by grooves round the top, as at Ickleton and Repton (31). Sometimes the shaft spread out a little like the mouth of a trumpet, as at Wittering. Very rarely the angles of the cap were covered with volutes and other motives from classical sources, but more often the cap was omitted altogether and a more or less elaborate and clumsy impost block was used instead (33).

Besides the circular shaft, turned moulded balusters, reminiscent of classic forms but exceedingly rude, were often used, particularly in twin-light windows, and especially in late, but not the very latest, work.

Big impost blocks (29, 32)—usually of square section, but occasionally roughly moulded with hollows and reeds—were very popular and characteristic.

WINDOWS.—Late pre-Conquest windows fall into three divisions. Firstly, a form which may be very early or very late, with the opening flush with the outer wall face, and splayed within ; the jambs slightly sloping towards one another with a lintel often cut into a semicircular arch (24), the jambs formed of large upright stones. Generally speaking, the early lights are fairly wide and very slightly splayed, the later very narrow and commonly splayed within.

The second form is splayed within and without; it is specially common where freestone is not obtainable, for instance in flint districts, where the arch was formed as it were in rough concrete. Often these openings are startlingly rough, and it seems probable that they were built on wicker basket-work centres. Very often they are circular. Many, but not all, of this type of window have a thin slab in the heart of the wall out of which the opening is formed. Often the opening is of a sort of rough keyhole shape, and it is very rarely of precise form.

The remaining type is that frequently used in the two-light openings to belfries, and consists of two arches, with square jambs and through arch stones, supported by a central shaft or baluster placed in the middle of the wall, carrying a long impost block (28). Earls Barton tower is distinguished by belfry windows of many lights, the shafts being turned balusters placed near the outer wall face, but this is exceptional (27). Windows of this type are rare in other positions but occur as an insertion in the west wall of Brixworth (2) and the north wall of the nave of Worth.

Circular windows were very commonly used in East Anglia, as at South Lopham and Coltishall, Cranworth tower and elsewhere. At Cranworth the opening was masked by a circular stone of carved open basket-work. They are rare in the West, but occur, very high up, in the naves of Bibury and Avebury.

In some small windows the opening is usually round-headed but sometimes very irregular, cut through a vertical slab set on the outer face of the wall, with rubble splays within. Instances occur of two-light windows of this sort—e.g., at Culbone, Somerset, and Daglingworth and Barnsley, Gloucestershire.

DOORWAYS.—The earlier pre-Conquest doorways were openings with square jambs, cutting straight through the wall without any provision for the door, which was hung on the inner face. But in later work there is usually a small check or rebate for the door. In the latest doorways the door is hung, as usual in post-Conquest work, somewhere about the middle of the thickness of the wall.

At Monkwearmouth one of the side doorways of the tower has large upright stones to form the jambs, and the arch is quite obviously made from the remains of two Roman arches, of the same span but of unequal depth, giving a curious lopsided effect. In the west door a more decorative effect was attempted. An upright and a flat stone, set long and short fashion, with crude carved relief ornament, form the lower part of each jamb. On these stand two turned baluster shafts, supporting a huge impost block, from which the flat semicircular arch springs. It was undoubtedly built in the seventh century, and foreshadows some of the features in common use in later times.

The jambs of pre-Conquest building are commonly constructed of slabs of the full thickness of the wall, alternately set upright and flat—long and short fashion ; or they may be of very large stones, or even of single stones. The impost block is usually very large. Sometimes it projects from the face of the wall (22), sometimes it does not.

The arch may be semicircular or triangular. If large stones are obtainable, these run through the full thickness, but this must not be expected in the stoneless districts.

The more elaborate doorways are usually framed by a flat pilaster strip in the fashion of a hood mould, following the curve of the arch and continued to the ground vertically (32). Usually the impost block projects sufficiently to stop the pilaster strip, but sometimes, particularly in the latest examples, the impost block is broken round the pilaster strip and may be moulded. There is an extreme irregularity in work of the late tenth century—for instance Earls Barton—but in the early ninth century the work is set out far more accurately. The effect is very decorative.

Any attempt at moulding the arch is rare and is no indication of date. Mouldings are crude, and have no trace of either Classic or Norman traditional formulæ, consisting of ill-combined rounds and sinkings, the rounds occasionally carved into cables.

Usually the opening is tall and narrow, and where Irish influence is strong the jambs may lean towards one another, as in the very primitive doorway of Somerford Keynes.

In the latest pre-Conquest doorways the impost block is much reduced in size and is sometimes moulded with some representation, in form approaching the Norman style, as at Daglingworth ; and the projecting pilaster strip is reduced in width till it becomes a hood mould not continued down the jambs, as at Deerhurst chapel.

Arches in two rings, flush with one another, occur in the seventh-century church of Brixworth (2, 26) and at Clee in work of a late period.

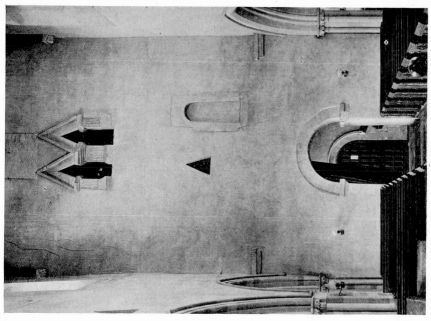

29 BRADFORD-ON-AVON, looking to the Chancel   30 DEERHURST, GLOUCESTERSHIRE: the west end

SAXON INTERIORS

31 THE SAXON CRYPT, REPTON, DERBYSHIRE

CHAPTER V

THE TRANSITION FROM SAXON TO NORMAN

It seems to be very generally believed that the Normans brought over a new style with them, ready-made and far superior to " Saxon."

This is an error. We have overrated the pre-Conquest architectural progress of the Normans and underrated that of the Saxons. Churches in Normandy which used to be regarded as pre-Conquest are now shown by competent antiquaries to be really of later date—notably the two abbey churches at Caen and St. Georges-de-Boscherville. There are very few pre-Conquest buildings in Normandy—Bernay, Jumièges and Cerisy-la-Forêt are the most important—and these are by no means so advanced in design as the early post-Conquest Winchester, Blyth, or Ely transepts.

If we examine a few English churches which are usually agreed to be of the time of Edward the Confessor, we find that considerable progress had been made by the later " Saxon " builders, and that they were by no means so backward as we used to believe. Undoubtedly the Normans had greater skill in stone-cutting, and their plans were often more ambitious, but the main characteristics of the Norman style were foreshadowed by our pre-Conquest work of the middle of the eleventh century. Some of it may have been influenced by the abbey church of Westminster, for which the Confessor imported Norman craftsmen, but the gradual evolution of the Norman style can be traced without a break by a comparison of English examples.

The main characteristic of Norman work is the use of the arch built in concentric overhanging rings, and the design of the pier or jamb in recessed faces with shafts to correspond with the compound arch it supports.

In a book which deals with parish churches the vault, on which modern antiquaries lay such stress, is comparatively unimportant, but it is well to bear in mind that in 1066 no high vault to a clerestoried building had been built in Normandy and that the barrel vaults of Monkwearmouth, Wing crypt and possibly Langford Tower are of earlier date than anything of the sort now existing in Normandy. Jumièges, St. Etienne and Caen only had groined vaults to the aisles. Repton crypt of the end of the tenth century had quite a decent groined vault (31). None of the Normandy groined vaults was earlier than 1050, and the Normans had not yet invented the ribbed vault; the honour of that discovery belongs to Anglo-Norman Durham.

The later development of Saxon work shows the gradual discontinuance of the large stone tradition, the evolution of the compound arch in concentric overhanging rings, and the appearance of a more definite type of capital.

The compound arch seems to have developed quite naturally from the use of pilaster strips framing the opening. It was but a small step to decorate the plain soffit of the arch with a similar pilaster strip. Pilaster strips of semicircular section were used in late tenth-century buildings—at Worth—and occur on the face of the arch at Wittering, and the substitution of a round for a flat pilaster strip resulted in such arches as Wittering, Boarhunt, Sompting, Wareham or Langford, which have the recessed arches, but are still in one ring. The unnecessary waste of stone, particularly evident at Sompting, led to the formation of the arches in two separate rings of stone, as at Langford.

The evolution of the jambs with clustered shafts is particularly well seen in a comparison of Wittering, Sompting and Bosham. Bosham, though certainly pre-Conquest, shows the usual Norman formula.

It is less easy to trace the source of the clustered shafts of the tower piers, as at Great Paxton and Ickleton, but the motive probably arose from multiplying the pilaster shafts.

At Great Paxton there are clustered shafts to the nave arcade of a type which hardly occurs in Norman work and is more characteristic of late twelfth-century work of the Transition, consisting of four engaged shafts with four roll mouldings between. Their capitals support arches in two orders, probably turned in brick.

It is also certain that the primitive method of constructing arches with voussoirs running right through the wall was giving place to a more economical method. Arches of such enormous thickness as Wing could not be so constructed without immense stones. The method was entirely dependent on the supply of large stones, and it cannot be expected in flint districts. Ickleton has an aisled and clerestoried nave and crossing of a character quite unlike Norman; it must be pre-Conquest. Here the arches are in a single ring, but mainly in rubble, with a small ring of stones to define the angles—quoin fashion.

Again, the more unusual forms of windows were dying out in the time of the Confessor, notably the double splay, and the small opening with a single splay was becoming much more common. Many of these exist, particularly in East Anglia, which show by the large stone technique and sloping jambs that they are not Norman work, but otherwise conform to the usual Norman type of the district.

As regards planning, the native tradition of the two-chambered church, separated by a narrow chancel arch (29), with the tower, if any, at the west, was strong enough to overwhelm any Norman tradition on the point. The eleventh-century parish churches of Normandy have either central towers or towers at the side of the chancel, very rarely, if ever, at the west end, and the separation between nave and chancel is much less pronounced.

Again, the single-chambered church of the Western Celtic tradition was usually adopted in those parts of the country where there was no tradition of a chancel arch, and is common enough in eleventh-century churches in the South-east, but unknown in Normandy. Above all, though all pre-Conquest churches in Normandy seem to have been apsidal, the native square end was employed in Anglo-Norman churches at least as frequently as the apse.

The pre-Conquest churches of Ickleton and Great Paxton show as full a development as any parochial buildings in Western Europe, with their central towers, transepts and aisled naves. The cruciform plan with central tower was already considered the normal for a large and well-staffed church, and had Harold's church at Waltham and Edward's church at Westminster come down to us, we should have been able to show great abbeys comparable to Bernay or Jumièges.

The strength of the native style is shown in the way pre-Conquest features persisted after the Conquest. For instance, the pilaster strip was not immediately dropped. It is found in twelfth-century work in the West Midlands. The tall towers with double light belfry windows, having a midwall shaft and long impost block, continued to be built on the old lines in Lincolnshire and persisted for a while in Northumbria.

Long and short quoins, on the other hand, do seem definitely to have been dismissed with the coming of the Normans, though they occur in the latest " Saxon " work.

The pre-Conquest builders seemed to find some difficulty with the design of capitals. The supply of Roman models had run short. The proper articulation of necking, bell and abacus had been forgotten. As we have seen, a great impost block—an exaggerated impost block—generally usurps the place of the capital (33). At Wittering the shafts swell into a hollow inverted bell below the impost block, while at Sompting a clumsy pseudo-Corinthian capital is attempted. At Bosham is something reminiscent of turned balusters, foreshadowing the moulded cap of the thirteenth century; here also we find a roughly circular abacus, again an anticipation of thirteenth-century style. Great Paxton shows circular bulbous capitals carrying a square abacus of a type unparalleled anywhere : a fine piece of experimental work, and the bases are of equally advanced design. At Repton we find cushion caps, very clumsy and the transition to the circular column badly botched (31), but at Ickleton, some hundred years later, the cushion cap is quite skilfully used to adapt the circular column to its square support, and except that the abacus is carved on the same stone, the form is like that used in some early Norman doorways.

The characteristic Anglo-Norman capital, the cubical, does not occur in Normandy before the Conquest, and though it may have come from Lombardy, it is more likely that it was discovered independently in England. The caps of the shafts to the belfry windows of the Lincolnshire group of

E

towers show its evolution, but not all of these are pre-Conquest. Something of the sort is used in the slight opening at the west end of Brixworth of the late tenth century (2).

To sum up, in the years immediately preceding the Conquest, " Saxon " architecture was developing rapidly into the style known as Norman, and it is highly probable that many features of the Anglo-Norman style were evolved not in Normandy but in England, and that the Normans adopted many forms hitherto unknown to them, which owe their origin to the Saxon craftsmen.

At the same time, extreme caution is necessary when assigning an approximate date to work of this period. Many examples of " Saxon " quoted in guidebooks are certainly post-Conquest. Herring-bone work especially is found in both late pre-Conquest and early Norman building, but is most frequent in the latter, and must not be taken as an indication of pre-Conquest date without other evidence.

33 THE SAXON TOWER ARCH, BARNACK

32 SAXON TOWER DOORWAY, EARL'S BARTON

34 BARFRESTON, KENT, THE SOUTH SIDE: a rich Norman village church

35 ADEL, YORKSHIRE: Norman, with later south windows and rebuilt gables, etc.

CHAPTER VI

THE NORMAN STYLE

INTRODUCTION.—The immediate effect of the Norman Conquest was to put a stop to most parish church building for some forty years, and thus to break the continuity of tradition. The actual Conquest was not simply a matter of winning the battle of Hastings. That victory made the ultimate result inevitable, but guerilla warfare went on for some time in outlying districts, and later there were revolts, punished in some instances, as Yorkshire, by the laying waste of the entire countryside.

Meanwhile all available labour must have been occupied in throwing up the mighty earthworks of the motte and bailey castles which sprang up, mushroom-like, in all parts of the kingdom, and formed an important element in the Norman scheme of conquest. These earthwork castles not only enabled a handful of Normans to overawe a far more numerous native population, but their construction, no doubt by Saxon labourers, must have done much to break the spirit of the vanquished.

This scheme of castle-building was astonishingly systematic, and was the outcome of the system of land tenure. The Conqueror had to pay his fellow-adventurers, and this he did in land. Those who had given the most valuable help naturally received the most. The land was already divided into estates, which the Normans called manors, and practically all was taken from the original owners, and dealt out to his own personal followers, on the condition that they should furnish the king with a specified number of armed men from each manor when called upon. These great barons in their turn distributed land to their own followers, and perhaps these again would give a portion of their holding to others, the condition being in each case that the sub-tenants should furnish a number of men for the army in proportion to the value of their land.

Finally, the lowest class of landholders was obliged not only to render military service, but also to give so many days' labour to their overlord in return for the holding.

Thus the whole country was organised on a military basis, and any new policy originating from the king quickly spread throughout the length and breadth of the land. The feudal system of land tenure undoubtedly contributed to the rapid spread of the newest ideas of building, particularly as the manors which fell to the share of one Norman baron were usually distributed over the country, perhaps in order to minimise the possibility of his mobilising an army against the king. On the other hand, it tended to

35

localise minor differences of style, for the lowest classes were " bound to the soil," and could not move permanently from one manor to another without the consent of their lord. From this class would come the labourers and wallers, while the skilled masons and carpenters must for the most part have been drawn from the small class of free men and were mostly of Norman birth.

The castles were at first mere field works, but as time went on many of them were consolidated by the building of permanent works in masonry, keeps, halls and walls of enceinte. The erection of these alone may well have employed the nation's builders for many years.

But the Normans were not only efficient soldiers. They were very zealous churchmen. Even before the military conquest of the country was complete, the colossal task of rebuilding the cathedrals and abbeys began, and in addition a very great number of new abbeys were founded. The fashion was set by the king himself, who founded the great abbey of Battle in thanksgiving for his victory, and the fashion passed from rank to rank right down the social scale. When we contemplate the vast body of Norman buildings still left and remember that only a very small part of the work done at this time has survived, it seems incredible that so great an enterprise could be the work of a population supposed to have been only about a couple of million.

The rebuilding of the greater churches seems to have been well in hand before such a general process of wholesale rebuilding was applied to the parish churches. Very early Norman work is common enough in cathedrals and abbeys, and not nearly so frequent in parochial building, but after 1100 the work of rebuilding the parish churches was accelerated. One of the results of the feudal system was that each lord of the manor was practically bound to provide a place of worship for his vassals, for it was not to his advantage for them to attend a church on an adjoining manor. It is useful to bear this in mind when visiting a Norman church. In all probability it was built at the cost of the lord of the manor, a proved soldier as well as a churchman, and in building it he had an eye to its possible military use in time of necessity, whether for himself and his followers in the event of a popular rising, or as a refuge for non-combatants if the manor should be in danger from a foreign invader or from a rival fellow-countryman. Few lords can have failed in this duty to their tenants.

Norman parish church building survives in a greater quantity in some districts than in others, but one is forced to the conclusion that there are very few churches in any part of the Norman sphere of influence which do not owe much to the work of this period. The quantity of surviving masonry may be small, and in many cases actual architectural features may be lacking, but it is a fact that nine out of ten of our churches grew up around a Norman nucleus.

We must not think of the Normans as bringing over a new style to

36

this country. Architecture had been developing rapidly in the West of Europe, on fairly uniform lines, since the year 1000. The Normans may have been a little in advance of the Saxons, certainly they were well ahead of the Ile de France, but England had been well abreast of Continental development in the days of the Confessor. It is likely that Edward's Westminster Abbey was, if anything, more fully developed than Jumièges or Bernay, and its plan was more ambitious. Normandy cannot now show buildings of pre-Conquest date so advanced in design as Great Paxton, Hadstock, Sompting, or the eleventh-century towers of Lincolnshire, which most modern antiquaries accept as pre-Conquest. The theory of the older Saxon style surviving after 1066, which once held the field, causing archæologists to look with suspicion on all buildings of " so-called Saxon " style and to post-date them, must give place to a more reasonable theory. We know that England was being Normanised before the Conquest and that she was in close touch with art development on the Continent.

The effect of the Conquest was to put an end to the lingering primitive tradition by its temporary check to church-building, and then to give an enormous impetus to the latest developments of architecture by the magnitude of the building enterprises of the conquering race. Saxon architecture would inevitably have developed on the lines of what we call the Norman style even if there had been no Conquest, but it would certainly have been less ambitious in its aims without the driving power of the Normans behind it.

The Norman system of building was essentially one of small stones and thick walls. Economy in worked stone, and a lavish waste of rubble, are its main characteristics. Just as the pre-Conquest builders delighted in huge stones, very heavy and difficult to transport to the building and to hoist into position, so the Normans seem to have derived equal pleasure from the construction of features, often overwhelmingly massive in effect, from a vast number of tiny blocks, each easily handled by one man. In the thickness of the walls, the numerous rings of the arches, the slight span of the openings, and the ample area of the supports, the Normans allowed a wide margin of safety; yet, in spite of the massive nature of their construction, and though their dressed stonework was often well and carefully wrought and jointed, their work often failed owing to the poor quality of the rubble and mortar.

Everything points to Norman work having been carried out in most instances by local unskilled labour, under the direction of one or more skilled masons. Only thus could such a vast amount of building have been executed by so small a population. As a matter of fact, the feudal system made it inevitable.

There are a few instances where this is not so evident. Such gems of Norman art as Barfreston (35, 39, 59) and Steetley or Adel (35, 62) seem to be almost entirely the work of skilled masons, but the theory of a few skilled masons directing a gang of unskilled local labourers holds good in the majority of cases.

We shall not go far wrong if we imagine the master mason with one or two apprentices arriving at the village, sketching out the general plan of the proposed building for the approval of the lord of the manor and his priest, and having sundry labourers from the village put under his charge. The master craftsman would peg out the building and set to work on the dressed stonework for quoins, doorways, windows and arches, while the local men were digging the foundations and building the thick walls. These would have an outer skin of fairly well-laid rubble walling and an inner skin substantial, but rough, since it was invariably plastered. This work would be done by such local men as had some knowledge of the art of walling, while the others poured into the heart of the wall a rough conglomeration of mortar and stones. Sometimes the mortar was fairly good, more often not, and in many buildings the heart of a Norman wall is a mere mass of stones and mud, which time has reduced to a fluid powder.

PLANNING.—Though many Norman churches stand on the site of Saxon buildings, it was customary to make a clean sweep of the old building and start entirely afresh.

The main types of Norman plans differ only in detail from those of the pre-Conquest churches.

At that period it was necessary to provide in every church (1) accommodation for the altar and those serving it, i.e., a sanctuary; (2) a space where the worshippers stood or knelt. Many of the smaller Norman churches were simply intended for the saying of Mass and had no other accommodation, but in more important places the choir office was said and a third space was needed, between nave and sanctuary, for those singing the office, i.e., a choir.

So a complete parish church then and throughout the Middle Ages demanded a tripartite plan of nave, choir, and sanctuary. Sometimes these divisions were marked architecturally, sometimes not.

We find sometimes (particularly in the West) a single-chamber plan, based on Celtic tradition; a plan which had little architectural dignity but which had the virtue of simplicity and eliminated the chief engineering problem of the Norman church builders, i.e., the construction of the chancel arch. It is impossible to be certain, but in most of these instances it is probable that there was no choir. The building was intended simply as a chapel for Mass.

More often the distinction between nave and chancel was marked architecturally by the latter being lower and narrower (34), and by a chancel arch, often extremely narrow. The chancel was sometimes only deep enough for a sanctuary, but in a few churches it is larger and was evidently intended to serve for both sanctuary and choir as at Wroxeter, Blockley, Warkworth.

37 ARCHES OF THE NORMAN CENTRAL
TOWER, STUDLAND, DORSET

36 THE NORMAN CHANCEL ARCH, GARWAY,
HEREFORDSHIRE

39 THE RICH NORMAN EAST FRONT,
BARFRESTON

38 BIRKIN, YORKSHIRE, FROM THE NORTH-EAST.
An apsidal tripartite Norman village church, with heightened tower
and Decorated tracery inserted in the east window

A few churches (Iffley and Stewkley are fine examples) had the tripartite division of the interior structurally marked (37), consisting of three chambers —a sanctuary, roughly square, a choir, also square and rather larger, and often surmounted by a tower, and a nave still wider, and at least twice as long as the breadth. Such churches were more difficult to build, since arches of fair span were necessary, and also more quoins and gable copings.

It is likely that few Norman parishes had more than one resident priest, but in larger places there were more, and it was necessary to provide more altars for these to say their daily Mass. These were usually accommodated by adding transepts to the choir space, producing the cruciform plan. Practically all really large Norman churches were planned in this way, though there are some very large ones which never had transepts—for instance, Much Wenlock. Even small churches had two side altars against the east wall of the nave, north and south of the chancel arch.

The population of Norman England was absurdly small in comparison with the enormous number of parishes and parish churches, and it was not often necessary to provide more space for the worshippers than a good-sized nave could afford. But in a few instances churches were built with aisles on each side of the nave (3). Usually these occur in towns which had recently grown up around some Norman stronghold.

Most of the ancient big towns got over the problem by the great number of their churches. A Norman church, built from the first with aisles to the nave, is a very great rarity, indeed, in this country, particularly as so many of the larger Norman churches have had to be enlarged and rebuilt in later times.

Still rarer are aisles to the choir. These were, of course, an alternative to transepts as a method of providing spaces for chapels. It seems to be an innovation in English parish church building, for no Saxon parochial chancels are known to have been aisled, though some had porticos. Norman examples are extremely rare and usually late. Ledbury seems to be a fairly early instance. Walsoken (3) is late twelfth century. In Northampton St. Peter we have a very rare example of a church with continuous nave, choir and sanctuary, both choir and nave aisled throughout. Such a plan is a Norman version of the early Basilican plan, with thicker walls, narrower spans and the apse omitted, but differing in no essential. However, it seemed to find no imitators until the end of the fourteenth century, when its possibilities were again explored and developed by the later Gothic builders.

Almost throughout Christendom the apse has been regarded as the right and proper ending to a church, but in England, on the fringe of Christianity, it was only adopted half-heartedly—probably owing very largely to lack of skill.

The Normans of Normandy regarded it as practically essential, but in England they seemed to have given way to the local tradition and to have built many more churches with square ends (34, 35) than with apses (38). So many of the Norman chancels have given place to longer ones of Gothic date that one cannot dogmatise, but it seems likely that apsidal endings were always in the minority, though in the flint districts the proportion of apsidal ends was much larger; for if an apse required more skill in the building, it saved the expense of wrought-stone quoins.

There are some instances of apsidal recesses for altars opening out of the east walls of transepts, but these are rare and have almost always been taken down. They are a commonplace of the Romanesque work of France. Shifnal is one example; Cuddesdon, New Shoreham, Bishops Cleeve, Melbourne, are others.

TOWERS.—The majority of Norman churches had no tower. The bells hung in small openings at the apex of the west gable, or, more rarely, on a gable above it.

When a tower was built it was often constructed over the choir. Most of the better Norman towers are in this position. But a good many were built at the west end of the nave, and are generally of huge bulk (40). Both of these positions have plenty of precedent in pre-Norman building. However, a number of Norman towers are not on the main axis of the church (41). In Cornwall there are several examples of early towers over the transept—and here and there one finds towers tacked on in the most curious positions—on the north side of the chancel (Chedgrave), on the south side of the chancel (Barford St. Michael), south of nave (Patrixbourne, Claverley), south of east end of nave (Alberbury), north of east end of nave. Most Norman towers are central and the next most favoured position was the west end.

Two western towers flanking the nave are occasionally, but very rarely, found, and usually denote some unusual constitution of the governing body. For instance, Melbourne, Derbyshire (on a manor of the Bishop of Bakewell); Reculver; St. Germans, Cornwall.

Norman towers (1, 41, 42) vary in character in different districts. In East Anglia the local circular slender form was adopted, as Little Saxham (42); in Lincolnshire the local tall rectangular campanile continued; but in Kent, Sussex (41) and the South-western counties the tower was generally of huge bulk—a keep rather than a campanile.

PORCHES.—Porches were not a feature of Norman planning. Bishop's Cleeve (9) and Bredon are authentic examples, but both are late in their period and must be regarded as exceptional.

VESTRIES.—It is usually stated that sacristies are not found in Norman plans, but at least two examples may be cited, that of Hemel Hempstead, with its charming vault, and Stanton St. Quintin in North Wiltshire.

CLERESTORIES.—Those Norman churches which were built with aisles seem all to have had clerestories. I do not know of a Norman nave with original aisles without some indication that there was a clerestory above.

40 THE NORMAN "TOWER-NAVE," FINGEST, BUCKINGHAMSHIRE

41 CLYMPING, SUSSEX   42 LITTLE SAXHAM, SUFFOLK

CONTRASTS IN NORMAN TOWER DESIGN

Norman nave clerestories remain at Sutton St. Mary, Whaplode, Walsoken (3), Steyning, Dover, St. Margaret's at Cliffe (43), and on a less elaborate scale at Overbury. Even the chancels, when aisled, as at St. Peter's, Northampton, Tilney All Saints, Walsoken and Ledbury, have clerestories.

ALTERATIONS TO PRE-CONQUEST BUILDINGS.—The first Norman builders usually made a complete clearance of any pre-existing church, and it is not usual to find work of the pre-Conquest and Norman periods in the same church. Nevertheless, instances of the alteration of a pre-Conquest building in Norman times do occur. A new doorway might be inserted in a nave, as at South Lopham, or a new tower arch in a western tower, as at Earls Barton, or larger arches inserted beneath a central tower, as at Cholsey.

In a few churches Norman arches of quite early date have been inserted in the walls of unaisled Saxon naves—for instance, at St. Nicholas, Leicester, and St. Michael, St. Albans, where the older windows are still visible above the arches, showing that aisles were added at this period—a practice which was afterwards to become more common.

Western towers were sometimes added to pre-Conquest churches; for instance, at Stottesdon, Compton, Womerston, and Saxthorpe, where the long and short quoins of the western angles of the nave are good evidence of pre-Conquest date, but the towers, though early, are of later work, showing no pre-Conquest features whatever. It is, however, far more common to find that a pre-Conquest tower has been heightened. This is particularly common in the round towers of East Anglia for instance.

Stow, Lincolnshire, is a rare example of a pre-Conquest cruciform church retaining its central crossing and transepts, but the nave and magnificent chancel were rebuilt on a larger scale by the Normans.

At Wroxeter a long late Norman chancel took the place of a short pre-Conquest structure, the older nave being retained.

ALTERATIONS TO NORMAN BUILDINGS.—But alterations were not confined to pre-Conquest buildings.

In late Norman times it was very usual to alter and enlarge quite recently erected churches of earlier Norman date, especially by the addition of aisles. When a Norman arcade is found on one side only of the nave, that is good evidence that it is an insertion, for it is safe to assume that a church would not be deliberately planned so unsymmetrically.

Often there are remains of the former side windows of the naves over these arcades, but while these are sometimes pre-Conquest, it does not follow that they are necessarily so. In many instances the windows are quite definitely of Norman style, showing that the original nave was post-Conquest and aisleless, and that the alteration has taken place within a few years of its first building. Examples are extremely common—Swalcliffe, Minster-in-Thanet, New Romney, are cases where aisles of more or less uniform design have been added on both sides; but more often the arcades differ decidedly in their details, while very frequently, as at Pittington and

F   41

Redbourne, only one aisle has been added. In fact, it may be proved that most Norman arcades are insertions in an earlier unaisled nave, and from this it may be gathered that unless it is certain that the church was originally built with aisles, the occurrence of a Norman arcade is strong evidence that the walls of the nave are of still earlier date.

Early Norman towers sometimes received an additional stage within a brief space. Castor (1) is a magnificent example of this, and here the upper stage was certainly not contemplated when the tower was first built. In any case, tower-building was slow work; the upper stages are often much later in style than the lower. Indeed some Norman towers offer in their successive stages a complete epitome of the development of style during the period.

An interesting and unusual case of alteration is that of Much Wenlock where the west façade was richly ornamented with arcading, the tower, apparently, having been planned on the south side. However, late in the Norman period the south tower was abandoned and a west tower built, completely obscuring the beauties of the older façade.

Yet another exceptional example of such alteration. The little church of Hampnet, Gloucestershire, was planned with a nave and separate chancel. In the latter part of the twelfth century an arch was built between choir and sanctuary and the latter covered with vaulting, thus turning the double-chamber plan into a triple-chamber.

WALLS.—Norman walls are usually at least 30 in. thick. Three-foot walls are common, and in large churches 3 ft. 6 in. or 4 ft. is not exceptional. Tower walls may be even as thick as 6 ft.

Only a very few churches of the period have any sort of base course. A chamfered offset is sometimes found, as at Iffley, and in very late Norman buildings quite a long slope, with a capping of semihexagonal section, may occur, particularly as a base to the buttresses or at the angles.

In the more pretentious Norman churches there was a string course under the window sills, within and without (34, 45), which has often survived when the original windows have long given place to larger openings (35).

Again, in the more elaborate churches a similar moulding was used as a hood mould and continued from one window to the other horizontally (34).

The treatment of the eaves illustrates a very characteristic, though by no means invariable Norman feature, namely, the corbel table, a series of projecting stones at intervals, carrying a continuous course of long flat stones, forming a fine cornice and giving the eaves greater projection (38, 43, 45). The corbels are generally carved into grotesques and the under side of the flat course is sometimes shaped into a series of semicircular arches. The corbel table is common in freestone districts, but was usually omitted elsewhere.

We have seen how the classic tradition of the division of a building into bays by means of pilasters was continued by the pre-Conquest masons. The

43, 44 ST. MARGARET'S AT CLIFFE, KENT, with its Norman clerestory

46 THE SOUTH NAVE ARCADE, MELBOURNE, DERBYSHIRE, with stilted Norman arcade

45 THE SOUTH SIDE OF THE NORMAN CHANCEL, NORHAM, NORTHUMBERLAND

Normans were addicted to the same practice where the necessary freestone was obtainable, but there was more system in their use of this feature, and their pilasters were usually, but not always, both wider and of greater projection. Though the spacing was generally irregular it was less erratic, and was occasionally used with some science to divide the church into bays. Such vertical pilasters, hardly worthy of the name of buttresses, are a feature of Norman building of the West Midlands, and occur sporadically in almost all districts where freestone is easily obtained (45).

Wider strips, practically shallow buttresses, but as a matter of fact adding very little to the strength of the wall, hugely thick in proportion, are not unusual in more important churches, particularly those which were intended to be vaulted; and these tended to become bolder as time went on and their abutment was appreciated. They sometimes finished under the corbel table, or were weathered on the top. The string courses sometimes ran round them (45), but they were always of the same projection throughout their height (38). In elaborate building, the angles of the buttresses were relieved by a small shaft set in a recess.

Buttresses of semicircular plan were not uncommon. They are very decorative, but of little practical use. Astley, Worcestershire, and Hanslope, Buckinghamshire, and Berkswell, Warwickshire, are examples. In the rebuilt tower of St. Peter's, Northampton, a cluster of three was applied to the western angles.

ARCHES.—The engineering problems involved in the building of a small Norman church were simple. Nothing revolutionary was ever attempted. The chief difficulty was the building of the chancel arch, and this could be reduced to a minimum by not attempting to span a wide opening. Consequently most Norman chancel arches are very narrow, but they were probably made as wide as the masons felt equal to building. Certainly they were made wider as their skill increased.

Like the pre-Conquest builders, the Normans knew only one form of arch, the semicircular, with its variants, the segmental (used when the height was limited) and the stilted (46) or horseshoe (which was employed when a taller arch was required). They occasionally employed a lintel over small openings, usually with a relieving arch above it. They seem to have rejected the triangular arch, though the form occurs as a sort of gabled hood mould over a doorway at Worth Matravers and Lullington.

The stones of a Norman arch never run right through the wall like those of pre-Conquest work. Though plain arches were often cut straight through the wall it was usual to confine the use of cut stone to the edges of the arch, to define the angle, quoin fashion, forming the rest of the arch in rubble (46). Such arches continued in use to the end of the twelfth century and perhaps later. They had the disadvantage of requiring elaborate wooden centering during their construction, for the whole thickness of the wall had to be provided with temporary support.

It was to avoid the use of such elaborate centering that the compound arch was evolved, and we have seen that the credit for this may be as much due to English enterprise as to Norman. The principle of the compound arch is to construct it in two or more concentric rings, the first, about half the total thickness of the wall, serving a centering for the second ring, which projected beyond the first. If the thickness of the wall demanded it, a third projecting ring could be laid without further centering. This construction was not only very strong but exceedingly effective, for each projecting ring casts a fine shadow on that below. Such an arch has a grandeur of its own even if it is left plain (44). When each ring is moulded or carved with contrasting motives the result is really splendid (3, 16, 36). In fact, the compound arch is the great glory of the Norman style.

Such an arch would look incongruous springing from square jambs or pillars, so these were built to suit the section of the arch in a series of recesses. The projecting angles were usually worked into slender shafts with capitals and bases.

Both methods, the simple and the compound arch, continued to be used all through the Norman style, and may occur in the same building.

SUPPORTS.—The plan of the support, whether the jamb of a chancel arch (36), the respond of an arcade, or the jamb of a doorway (62), had to be designed with reference to the section of the arch it was intended to support. Simple arches usually had plain square jambs, but often the angle was worked into a slender shaft with capital and base. A similar treatment was applied to the detached pillars of arcades such as that at Rainham, Kent, and Enford. Compound arches required jambs worked with a series of recesses, and each of the angles might be worked into a shaft, or a detached shaft might be inserted to carry each ring of the arch. This is very common in chancel arches and responds, and in doorways (60). A great variety of effect was obtained by working shafts to support certain of the arch rings, allowing the rest to run down to the floor. The pillars of an arcade are rarely treated thus, but examples occur at St. Mary's, Dover, and Polstead. More often they are circular in section, and sometimes octagonal. At Walsoken the two forms are used alternately (3).

Classic tradition demanded that an isolated support should be a column, circular in section, with a capital, a base and an abacus. Norman columns and shafts are based on classic tradition; the base, usually simply moulded and standing like the classic base on a square plinth, was a modification of the classic Attic base, but as the column was of greater diameter and consequently much heavier, the moulding was flattened and spread, as if it were in truth the Attic base actually compressed by the huge weight it carried.

PIERS.—When the Normans wished to provide a detached support for two arches, their preference was for a circular pillar (46). If the pair of arches were those of a double window to a tower (55), a monolith shaft of circular section was employed; or if the weight to be carried were small, the pillar would be built in a series of stone drums—but more often the pier was absurdly large in proportion to the load, and was built in courses of small stones with a rubble core. It is rare to find clustered shafts in the arcade of a parish church, though they were common enough in cathedrals and abbeys. They may be regarded as a couple of shafted jambs of the normal type placed back to back. A square block of masonry is a usual form, and the bluffness of such a support was often relieved by cutting the angles into the form of shafts with capitals and bases.

Oddly enough most of the examples of this type occur in rather late Norman or Transitional work, though the effect is decidedly primitive.

The capital is merely a device to adapt the circular plan of the column to the square arch it supports. Even the elaborate Corinthian (50) or Composite caps are no more than this. In Norman work the favoured cap was in outline the simplest form which would meet the case—the cushion cap is simply a cylinder spreading out into a square prism or a cone intersecting with a square prism. It was capable of elaborate treatment with surface ornament, and was often elaborately carved (53). Some capitals, like those in the west front of Leominster, are impressionistic versions of the Corinthian cap, retaining in some instances only the volutes at the angles and the block representing the classic rose in the centre of each side below the abacus. Very rarely one finds all the elements of the Corinthian caps reproduced extremely clumsily, usually in early work.

The abacus or impost was hardly ever omitted. Artistically it rules a line of shadow at the junction of the arch and its support; practically, it served as a support for the wood centering on which the arch was constructed. In section it was rounder than the great impost blocks of the Saxons, and was usually moulded according to several very constant types, which, however, developed gradually; and therefore the abacus is a good index to date—usually the upper angle is square, the lower slightly hollow-chamfered, with a V-shaped groove at the intersection (48). The relative size of vertical face and the chamfers are excellent indication of date. If the vertical face is deep, it is probably early work, and the narrower the vertical face, the later it is.

Such was the Norman column, a massive, impressionistic version of the classic column. But it was used in a much more slender form to decorate the angular faces of jambs of arches, the angles of buttresses or window splays; and eventually this led to a modification in the section of the arch rings. In the earliest work the rings of the arches are of square sections, though they may be elaborately decorated with surface ornament, but in later work the section of the arch was often modified to echo the section of the jambs and sometimes even to reproduce it, adding to the general effect of richness and to the play of light and shade.

WINDOWS.—Pre-Conquest windows had been of three types: (1) openings cut straight through the wall; (2) windows narrow without and widely splayed within; and (3) windows with both external and internal splays. That seems to have been the order in which they were inserted, but some time before the Conquest the second type, with internal splay only, was beginning to find favour, and the Normans used no other.

It was not an easy form to construct. In the first place, though the external arch was often so small that it required no centering—being in one, two, or at the most three stones—the wide internal splay needed an elaborate centering. This must inevitably have been composed of three wood semicircles, each of different span, boarded over, and the back board must have been tapered to suit the conical surface.

In the plainer churches the external arch was in wrought stone, but the internal arch was in rubble, save for a ring on the inner side to strengthen the intersections of splay and wall—quoins, as it were, bent to the curve of the arch; but where freestone was plentiful the whole arch was in wrought stone. The masoncraft required for such work was of no mean order.

Norman windows fall into two classes : (1) small unglazed openings (56); (2) large windows evidently intended to be glazed (45). The former are by far the most numerous, for it is certain that the almost unbelievable smallness of the prevailing type of window was due to the fact that larger openings, while letting in more light, would have let in also more cold air. The notion of defence was not absent, but the scarcity and high cost of glass was an even more urgent factor. Only rich churches could afford glass, and therefore the average Norman parish church was a very gloomy and draughty place, lit only by a few very small and narrow openings, widely splayed within. The arches are almost always semicircular and the jambs perfectly upright. Proportions varied greatly, but generally they were somewhat squat. The treatment of the exterior of such slits is generally as simple as could be, the jambs square and unmoulded, the arch generally worked in a single stone (56). Late in the twelfth century such openings were generally chamfered, or chamfered and recessed.

The large windows, intended for glazing, were usually treated externally exactly like a little doorway, with two orders to the arch, and perhaps shafts with caps and bases to the jambs (57, 58), and almost always a hood mould of some kind. Internally there is sometimes only a plain splay, but occasionally the intersection of splay and wall face may be moulded, or the interior may be treated like the exterior with moulded arch and shafted jambs. But such elaborate treatments are rare, except in districts where freestone was plentiful.

Circular windows are not uncommon, particularly in clerestories (Ledbury) and at the east or west ends (Iffley, and St. James's, Bristol). They very rarely occur in side walls—as in the church of Haddiscoe. At Barfreston (39) and Castle Hedingham the large circular opening is filled in with an arcade radiating from the centre, i.e., traceried. At Cuckmer a circle is

47, 48 DUCKLINGTON, OXFORDSHIRE

49 WALSOKEN, NORFOLK

50 ST. WOOLOS, NEWPORT,
MONMOUTHSHIRE

51 BARTON-LE-STREET,
YORKSHIRE

52 EASINGTON, COUNTY
DURHAM

NORMAN CAPITAL DESIGN

53　THE CHANCEL ARCH, WAKERLEY, NORTHAMPTONSHIRE

54　THE CHANCEL ARCH, ADEL

cusped. Practically always, and especially in early work, no attempt at grouping was made, and then only at the east and west ends—but occasionally one meets delightful groups of Norman windows, sometimes skilfully combined as in the west fronts of Iffley, Castle Rising, or on a less ambitious scale at Malinslee.

Position.—Norman windows, especially the long unglazed ones, were placed high up in the walls (34), and as a rule they were as few in number as possible. There was no attempt at bay design and, rarely, at equal spacing. In small churches in the Midlands the north wall was devoid of windows, and very few naves possessed more than three on each side, while a couple in each side wall is a liberal allowance for a chancel of fair size, though in a few large choirs the provision was more liberal and there were sometimes three or more. The east end was sometimes blank, as at Notgrove, Cold Aston, Brimpsfield, or there was a single tiny light—Elkstone, Heath Chapel, Hampnet. Examples of groups of several windows, often with a circular light above, occur, as at Rainham, or a pair with a niche between, as at Malinslee, but these are rare. At the west end groups of three or four (16), sometimes with a circle introduced, are less unusual, but most churches had but one. Generally speaking, groups of Norman windows are likely to be of later date than single lights, but the device was adopted quite early. It was nothing new. Grouped tiers of windows had been used for years in the west fronts and transept ends of the greater churches.

DOORWAYS.—These were as a rule the most elaborate features of a small Norman church. Practically every church had a north door and south door to the nave, placed as a rule fairly near the west end, while many had a western doorway in addition. A few of the larger chancels also had a priest's door on the south side, rarely, if ever, on the north, and near the west end of the chancel (34). Some of the large cruciform churches also had doorways at the ends of the transept, as at Bampton, or on the west face of the transept.

The system of construction employed differs a good deal from that employed in pre-Conquest doorways. These, as we have seen, consisted of an archway cut straight through the wall, with the door hung against the inner face, or in comparatively small rebates. The Norman practice was to hang the door nearly in the centre of the wall and to treat the inner and the outer half of the doorway quite differently. The outer half of the opening was rather narrower than the inner to form a rebate for the door, and the inner half of the arch was taken up much higher to allow the doors to open. The outer half had an arch in one or more rings, usually recessed, and the jambs corresponded ; but the inner half, or rere-arch, was severely plain, and generally dressed stone was confined to one ring on the inner face of the wall, the rest of the soffit being in rubble.

Probably two wood centres were employed in their construction, one a stout arch built up of wood for the first ring of the outer arch, and one composed of two wood arches boarded over to support the rubble soffit.

47

The change in construction did not necessarily come in the mathematical centre of the wall. In the simpler doorways the outer arch is not more than about eight inches thick and all the rest is rere-arch, while in elaborate doorways with several overhanging rings the rere-arch is of very slight width.

A few Norman doors are extremely simple (45)—some have square jambs and a deep square lintel, which may be plain (Little Wratting) or the form of a semicircular arch may be carved upon it. Others have plain jambs and a plain arch. The hood mould is often omitted, but practically always imposts were provided. Most of these simple doorways are early work, but some are certainly late. While the treatment of the doorway certainly tended to become more and more elaborate, it was the means of the builders, rather than the fashion of the moment, which decided the question. Many of the doorways were very richly ornamented even if only with simple square jambs and arch, but in most the elaborate effect was attained by means of the characteristic formula of the style—the use of concentric rings to the arch, each succeeding ring projecting above that below, and the treatment of the jambs to correspond, as at Adel (61) and Chepstow (16).

One finds arches in two, three, four, and sometimes even five or six rings (16), and in some instances the wall may have had to be thickened to accommodate the great depth of the doorway recess. Each succeeding ring was treated in a different manner. A ring might be left plain, or moulded with the simple rounds and hollows in vogue, or it might be carved with the fashionable zigzags or with any of the varied motives drawn from the many sources which the Norman carvers had at their command (Barfreston, 57). The capitals could be covered with surface ornament, the impost mould and hood mould were often enriched with carving, and even the jamb shafts were often encrusted with rich decoration (Adel, 61), and the bases had a leaf ornament to fill in the space between circular shaft and square plinth.

In many examples the actual opening is square, the first order of the jambs supporting a semicircular lintel (tympanum) (59, 60) about which the succeeding rings of the arch are built. Variants of this method are found; sometimes there is a lintel, with the tympanum filled in with a slab, or with stones laid in a geometrical pattern, while some of the lintels are really flat arches in several stones with radiating or joggled joints. At this period the use of two contrasting stones is often found, adding to the effect of barbaric richness—at Paignton red sandstone and white beerstone, at Tredington white limestone and grey lias, and so on.

ORNAMENT.—With a very few exceptions Norman ornament is in low relief, carved out of the surface, never standing clear of the architectural feature it adorns. The greatest care was taken to occupy every bit of the vailable space.

The peculiarity of the style is the use of purely geometrical ornament,

55 BRAYTON TOWER, HEREFORDSHIRE

56 ADEL

57 KILPECK, HEREFORDSHIRE

58 BIRKIN

NORMAN WINDOW DESIGN

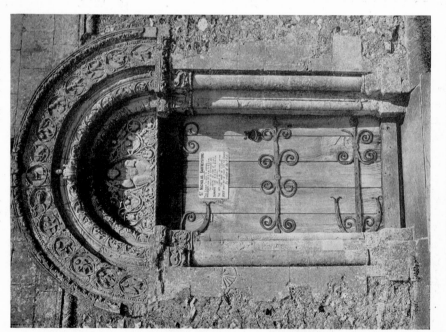

60 THE SOUTH DOOR, ELKSTONE, GLOUCESTER-
SHIRE, with Norman chevron and beak-head ornament

59 THE SOUTH DOORWAY, BARFRESTON,
with elaborate Norman carving

such as the billet (55), formed by working a round moulding and cutting portions away; the pellet, little round beads (58); the zigzag (60, 62); and the sunk star. The origin of this geometrical ornament is somewhat obscure, probably Scandinavian, but everything was grist to the mill of the Norman carver.

From Celtic and Irish sources came the use of interlacing stems—a sort of basket-work in stone (57). There are reminiscences of classic tradition in the use of volutes at the angles of capitals and in some of the leaf scrolls.

The beak head (60, 61) is one of the most effective motives of the period, marvellously widespread, yet of no definite ancestry. It seems to be a development of the geometrical species of zigzag, the triangles of which irresistibly suggest the idea of adding eyes and ears.

Manuscripts of all dates were drawn upon for inspiration and from these came the scenes of medallions (59) with signs of the zodiac, as at Iffley—the beasts of the bestiaries, as at Alme—and some of the more accomplished running scrolls.

Figure sculpture was used sparingly and was usually Byzantine in feeling, probably inspired by imported ivory carving. The subjects were few. Christ in Majesty is often represented in tympana (59), sometimes surrounded by the Apocalyptic beasts, as at Elkstone (60); the Harrowing of Hell is frequent. The Virgin and Child and the Coronation of the Virgin are rarer, but the former occurs at Quenington. St. Peter is represented at Handborough, St. George at Fordington.

Samson and the Lion were distinctly popular, occurring, for example, on a tympanum at Highworth, Wilts., but Old Testament subjects are rare.

Many figure subjects are entirely secular. If a figure is represented between two griffins the probability is that the carver intended to represent the miraculous flight of Alexander—a popular romance. The Normans were good soldiers and loved a fight, so we get contests between centaurs, centaurs and dragons, as at Adel (54), knights and lions, as at Iffley.

The science of iconography had not yet been systematised as it was in the thirteenth century. It would be wrong to believe that every Norman carving had some spiritual meaning; it is equally wrong to suppose that it had none.

One very striking feature of Norman architecture is that as a rule each stone was treated individually; each stone had its own repeat of the ornament. If one stone was smaller than the other the ornament was spaced to suit it. This gives a delightful effect of freedom. A marvellous effect of richness was obtained by combining these motives together. The technique is always highly conventional. The notion of inspiration from nature hardly occurred to the carver save in some of his spirited carvings of contests.

Roofs.—It is possible that some Norman roofs may survive in a much repaired condition, but it is impossible to cite examples with any confidence.

The marks of former roofs against towers often give the pitch, and as the carpenters' methods altered very little throughout the thirteenth and fourteenth centuries, and the old forms persisted side by side with newer ones in the fifteenth, it is reasonable to suppose that twelfth-century roofs were not unlike those of the thirteenth century.

But the frequent survival of doorways, high up in gable walls, the sill on a level with the wall-plate, indicates that flat ceilings were frequently used, a relic of those of Early Christian basilicas. Otherwise it is difficult to explain why these doorways should have been provided unless they led to a floor above a flat ceiling. Where a flat ceiling survives in connection with a Norman fabric the effect is very happy. These flat ceilings certainly had a gabled roof over.

In less important churches, where every bit of height helped to give dignity, it is likely that the roof was exposed internally.

Two primitive forms of roof which we find in later work were probably employed in Norman churches. (1) The so-called trussed rafter roof, in which each pair of rafters is strengthened by collars, by ashlar pieces, rising from the wall-plate, level with the wall face, and by inclined struts between the rafters and the collar.

In a roof of this sort each pair of rafters may be regarded as a wooden arch, tending to thrust the walls apart. As they are set close together the thrust may be regarded as distributed along the whole length of the wall, needing continuous thick walls to resist the outward pressure. Tie-beams at intervals were sometimes used to prevent the wall-plates being thrust apart.

(2) A simple form of tie-beam roof may have been employed. In a roof of this sort, strong triangular frames (principals) are set at intervals of seven to ten feet, supporting beams, known as purlins, running from end to end of the building. These in their turn support the rafters, which need not be strengthened by collars and struts. Such a roof has no thrust, but reduces the apparent height of a building. The lean-to roofs over aisles were usually so narrow that no strengthening was necessary for the rafters.

All other Norman roofs were gabled, the pitch being usually as low as the roofing material allowed. For thatch it might be as much as 55°, but for heavy stone slabs it was not more than about 40°. Something between 45° and 50° is the most usual.

62 THE SOUTH DOORWAY, ADEL, with
elaborate Norman zigzag patterning

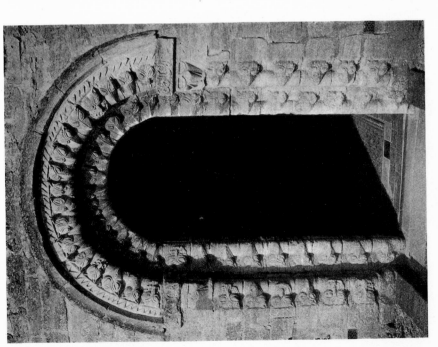

61 THE SOUTH DOORWAY, WINDRUSH, GLOUCES-
TERSHIRE, with Norman beak-heads

63 BATTLE, SUSSEX

64 MOULTON, LINCOLNSHIRE

TRANSITIONAL INTERIORS

CHAPTER VII

THE TRANSITION FROM NORMAN TO EARLY ENGLISH

IN the sixty years between 1100 and 1160 fashion changed almost imperceptibly. Certainly there was a tendency, perhaps due to the influence of Cluniac churches, to a greater richness in detail, but simplicity or elaboration is not a safe guide to date. Richness of detail depended on the funds available rather than the vogue of the day. Plain Norman work may be early or late; elaborate Norman work is usually fairly late. The degree of relief in the carving is a good indication of date—if shallow, it was probably cut with an axe and is likely to be before 1120; but if deep or undercut, it was certainly carved with a chisel and cannot be earlier than 1100.

Of improvement in construction there is little sign. Certainly masons became a little bolder in throwing arches across wider spans, and there was a tendency to reduce the size of supports, and even a growing willingness to attempt the construction of vaults over, at least, parts of the church. But for a while architecture was content to go on in the old way, and though each building was an improvement on its predecessor, there was no startling change of fashion.

Then, in the middle of the twelfth century, development quickened its pace. A far-reaching invention was that of the pointed arch. Already many of the less carefully built Norman arches were failing. Jambs had spread and crowns of arches sunk, and this was due not only to bad building but to the inherent weakness of the semicircular arch. The haunches of the arch did not fail, the radiating joints were so nearly horizontal, and the friction between the arch stones so great, that there was no thrust worth mentioning from this portion of the arch—the first few stones would stand up by themselves. It was in the crown of the arch that the weakness lay; the joints nearly vertical, each stone a wedge forcing the abutments apart, and no friction to speak of between arch stone and arch stone, as the pull of gravity was in the direction of the joint. The Norman builders, practical fellows in spite of their faults, must have seen that the flat crown was the weak part of the semicircular arch. If that could be eliminated the thrust would be reduced; and if we eliminate the crown of a semicircular arch we get a pointed arch, a stronger form of arch altogether, exercising much less thrust, and one which, unlike the semicircular arch, could be made as high or as low as the builder desired. The greater the rise, the less the thrust. But to men who had only known the semicircular arch, its form must have seemed bizarre, even ugly and disjointed. For some time it was chiefly used as a structural expedient to reduce the thrusts of arches of wide span (3, 15), or those bearing a heavy weight, such as tower arches, while the semicircular arch was retained for smaller openings. There is very little doubt that the change of the form of arch was largely due to the influence of the early Cistercian churches, which introduced the latest Burgundian ideas into England, and at the same time influenced the ornamental system. Hitherto the barbaric splendour of the Cluniac style had had the strongest influence on parish church building. After 1160 the severe Cistercian style was more influential. In the latest Norman churches, apart from the change in the form of the arch, one finds more reticence in the ornament; plain mouldings take the place of carved voussoirs, plain scalloped, plantain or water-leaf caps, simple and elegant, but severe (52), occur where in earlier days we should have found clumsy caps, their barbarous shape camouflaged by the richness of the surface ornament.

A change was coming over the whole country. The Norman and the Saxon races had fused. A new nation had come into being. The social distinctions of the Feudal system were beginning to level out. The freedom of the individual was beginning to be recognised as an ideal worth striving for, which won its first genuine victory in the sealing of Magna Charta, and a vast change in the ownership of land had taken place owing to the extensive endowment of abbeys. A very considerable portion of the country was now in the hands of the Church. While in the Norman period the lord of the manor had been a little king, lording it over his tenants and patronising the Church, and more or less dictating the character of the churches, now the bishop or abbot was a greater landholder than most lay lords and had more say in the matter than they.

Now the late twelfth century was in the Church the great age of liturgical development. The older liturgical customs were taught, elaborated and systematised and put into writing. One church vied with another in the orderly beauty and magnificence of its services. The movement was bound to spread to the parish churches.

Certainly towards the end of the twelfth century the main influence on church architecture was ecclesiastical rather than military. Churches became more spiritual in feeling. The secular motives in the sculpture which had appealed to the lover of hunting or fighting such as the old patrons of church building were, died out in favour of simple foliage of no particular significance, but chaster and severer in effect. If there was little direct symbolism in the ornament, at least it did not distract the minds of worshippers from heaven to earth.

The pointed arch was lighter in effect than the semicircular, and the effect of lightness was enhanced when it was understood that with less thrust to be anticipated from the arch its supports could be made lighter.

Yet another cause operated in favour of the change of style. It has been emphasised that few Norman windows were intended to be glazed.

65 SOHAM, CAMBRIDGESHIRE

66 CANON PYON, HEREFORDSHIRE

TRANSITIONAL ARCADES

67 FARINGDON, BERKSHIRE. The Transitional nave arcades

Glass was scarce and costly, and windows had to be kept as small as possible, and interiors were gloomy from necessity, not choice. Now it is certain that in the latter part of the twelfth century the manufacture of glass developed and it began to be within the reach of even small churches. No longer need the windows be made so small and few. At last the church could be made lighter, without admitting all the winds of heaven. Some glazing of the period survives, and most windows show, by their glazing grooves, that they were intended for glass; but still in many remote places windows were still unglazed.

Another factor tended to improve the lighting of the parish church, namely, the more settled state of the country. Life in the late twelfth century was still somewhat precarious, but the chances of reaching a ripe old age were certainly more rosy than in the middle of the tenth. At least Viking raids had ceased. There was little fear of foreign invasion, and though there had been the anarchy during the contention of Stephen and Maud for the throne—a ghastly period of some nineteen years—under Henry II. the feudal laws had been enforced, and as a whole the country was fairly safe for the law-abiding citizen. Except on the Welsh or Scottish borders and on the coast, the probability of the church being required as a place of refuge was remote. It was no longer necessary to place windows very high up, or to make them so narrow that a man could not pass through them, and so windows began to be elongated, and in some districts widened as well.

Another factor in the change of style was the increase of skill in mason-craft. The rule-of-thumb methods of the pre-Conquest and early post-Conquest days were giving place to more mathematical accuracy. Mason-craft was still very free and easy; exact symmetry and precision were not overrated, but arches and their supports—abacus, capital, base and shaft—were brought into closer relationship and more logically worked out. More accurately worked joints and finer jointing resulted in less settlement and greater stability. Stone quarrying during the twelfth century must have advanced considerably in answer to the huge demand for freestone, and no doubt methods of transport improved. Certain it is that in buildings of the late twelfth century we find larger blocks employed than in the beginning of the century. The unmistakable Norman technique of facing with almost cubical blocks gives place to longer stones and higher courses, more finely jointed; and even in rubble work more care is observed in the coursing. In East Anglia, on the other hand, the carefully coursed flint work in unsplit flints gives way to a rougher technique.

But the most striking feature of the period is the greater depth of cutting due to the use of the chisel instead of the axe. Where shallow relief work would have been employed in earlier work, the foliage under the chisel rises from the surface and takes life and sprouts from the stone instead of lying inert on the face of the block. Many Transitional arcades show the evolution. One column may have a purely geometrical scalloped cap (65), the next has a graceful curve to the cones, which separate till they become cornucopias, sprouting into foliage (72), while in the next the husk has been shed and the foliage in vigorous growth stands alone (73).

The distribution of Transitional work of the twelfth century is very curious. It is common in the Midlands, the South-east (63) and the North-east (64), but almost unknown in Norfolk and Suffolk, Lancashire and Cheshire, exceedingly rare in Somerset, Devon and Cornwall, and uncommon in Dorset. In Northamptonshire and the adjoining counties good examples abound, and in North Berkshire (67) and West Oxfordshire it is perhaps commoner than pure Norman.

Making allowance for the extensive buildings of the fourteenth and fifteenth centuries in those counties where it is rare, it is still clear that most of the prosperity of the country at this time was concentrated in the Midlands and the South-east and North-east.

Little nave-and-chancel churches continued to be built, especially in the South Midlands, but generally show much longer proportions. The chancels, especially, are often of considerable length.

Great aisled churches were often undertaken as complete schemes, as at Castle Hedingham and Ramsey. They are particularly to be noted on the Welsh border, for instance at Bosbury, Ripple, etc., and in the North, that is, in the last portions of the country to be definitely held by the Normans.

At Tilney All Saints and Emneth the chancels also had aisles and clerestories, and in the first instance the chancel arch is omitted.

Very many churches were laid out with central towers, a deep chancel, transepts and aisled nave, as St. Mary's, Shrewsbury, Lambourne and Faringdon, Berkshire (67), where Norman churches were almost completely cleared away for the new constructions.

At Cuddesdon aisles to the nave were omitted, but there were chapels projecting east of the transepts.

The type having a central tower but no transepts still persisted, as at Bredon, but was giving way to the simpler two-chambered plan in smaller churches.

As yet transeptal chapels were very rarely undertaken, but there are a number in Cornwall which seem to be of late twelfth-century date.

Most Transitional work was built in alterations to existing Norman or pre-Conquest churches. Probably more than half the remaining work of this date in parish churches is to be found in arcades, showing that the addition of aisles was becoming extremely popular. The original aisles, being very narrow, have usually given place to later building. They were normally covered by an extension of the nave roof, and had very low side walls and small windows, and consequently darkened the nave excessively.

Norman naves were lengthened at this period, as at Whaplode.

Porches, which were not employed in Norman parochial work, began

69　COTES-BY-STOW, LINCOLNSHIRE

68　CUDDESDON, OXFORDSHIRE

TRANSITIONAL DOORWAYS

70 LITTLE FARINGDON,
OXFORDSHIRE

71 POLEBROOK,
NORTHAMPTONSHIRE

72 FARINGDON, TOWER ARCH

73 TILNEY ALL SAINTS, NORFOLK

TRANSITIONAL CAPITAL DESIGN

to be built, as at St. Mary's, Shrewsbury, and Witney, and two, at least, of these, Bishop's Cleeve (9) and Bredon, have upper stories.

Tower building went on slowly, and few parish churches yet possessed towers. Garsington is a good example.

DOORWAYS follow the Norman formula as to their recessed and shafted jambs and the general square section of the arch-stones, but the arch may be pointed or semicircular, and the decoration of the caps and capitals of the shafts is usually of foliage form (68), the older cubical and cushion caps having fallen into disuse, and the mouldings may be plain or enriched with the Norman zigzag in a developed and undercut form (68). The Early English dog-tooth was first used in this period, a series of contiguous square pyramids, ruched out into petals at the base (68, 89).

WINDOWS of the Transitional period are rare. Often they are like the small Norman ones, but with a chamfer round the opening. Sometimes the arch is circular, with the arch of the splay pointed, or the reverse may occur.

Generally they are longer than Norman windows of the same class and often they are taller in proportion. A recess and chamfer is a favourite treatment in the South Midlands.

In more elaborate churches they may have shafted jambs either within or without, following the Norman formula, but with the newer treatment of the caps, bases, abacus and arch mould. The pointed and the semicircular arch are used at will and are often combined.

The ARCADES and CHANCEL ARCHES of this period (63-67) are among the most beautiful and interesting in England. It is curious to see how sometimes, as at Great Bedwin, Wilts., the piers are more advanced in design than the arches and sometimes the reverse is the case. We meet with piers of almost purely Norman form carrying pointed arches (65) having little trace of Norman style, and on the other hand, particularly in Northampton-shire, we find piers of the newer style carrying round arches.

The normal PILLAR of a small parish church was still the cylindrical pier of circular section but the octagon was beginning to be equally popular. A cluster of four shafts is not uncommon—square with shafts on the angles. Bases are of wide spread, often on square chamfered plinths, and a leaf is often introduced at each angle to fill in the blank space. The section tends to the Early English water-holding base, but is generally flatter.

CAPITALS (70-73) are sometimes in earlier work of the scalloped form, but tend to be of hollowed profile instead of swelled or straight. Often these break out into foliage. The water-leaf cap and plantain-leaf cap are typical, and so is one composed of grotesques and foliage, a compromise between the Norman and Early English motives.

The ABACUS is usually either polygonal (67, 70) or square (71-73) on plan, never circular, and the upper edge is usually square in section, though in very late Transition it may be rounded. The section varies from a close approximation to the Norman " quirk and chamfer " (73) to the Early English undercutting (64, 67).

The ARCHES are in one or two orders and, if plain, the edges are usually chamfered off (64); the later the work, the wider the chamfer (66), but they may be enriched with zigzags and other Norman ornaments, but much refined and usually deeply undercut—or they may be moulded (67), the members following the original square section of the voussoirs very closely.

The pointed arch by itself does not constitute the Transitional style. It is used in work otherwise pure Norman, early examples being the vault of Durham and the arcades of Buildwas. Walsoken, for instance (3, 49), is pure Norman save for the form of the chancel arch.

Again, Norman arches were rebuilt in the pointed shape long after their erection, owing to the failure of the flatter semicircular arch, sometimes with the old voussoirs, as in the chancel arch of Wakerley—often with entirely new stonework in the style of the day, as at Blockley—both of these being purely Norman works. Again, a Norman chancel arch was sometimes taken out, a larger arch being inserted in its place, the old work being utilised in one of the arches of the nave arcade, in a pointed shape, as at Sutton Courtney.

Most of the CARVING is concentrated on the capitals and it is much more sparsely used. The scallop cap of the previous period lingered on, but was hollowed out and undercut; the semicircular lobes often become complete circles, decorated with trefoil foliage, getting more and more free, until they become cornucopias, sheathing trefoiled foliage. The beautiful water-leaf cap, apparently introduced by the Cistercians, was very popular, and so was the plantain leaf (72). The tendency was to discard grotesques, basket-work and geometrical motives and adopt a more naturalistic treatment of foliage (70-73).

A typical Transition base standing on a big square plinth is often relieved by spurs springing from the moulding to each angle. These may take the form of grotesque dragons, plantain leaves, water-leaves or rather bold and crude precursors of the stiff-stalked trefoil foliage of the succeeding style.

Figure work is extremely rare.

74 LITTLE FARINGDON, OXFORDSHIRE: an untouched Early English Chancel

75 THE SOUTH SIDE OF THE EARLY ENGLISH CHANCEL,
ROTHBURY, NORTHUMBERLAND

76　FILEY, YORKSHIRE, FROM THE SOUTH-EAST : an Early English cruciform church with central Tower

CHAPTER VIII

THE EARLY ENGLISH STYLE

INTRODUCTION.—By the last decade of the twelfth century the first of the Gothic styles had fully developed, though the Norman tradition died hard and sundry details and methods lingered on for perhaps twenty years more. Gothic came to birth at a time which the history books regard as far from prosperous—the reigns of Richard and John. Henry III., on the other hand, was a patron of the arts, and much of the best work was probably done in his long reign, in spite of the Civil War of Simon de Montfort. The dispute with the Pope in 1207, the interdict, 1208-1213, resulted in the complete defeat of the King by the Church. Ecclesiastical influence was far stronger than regal or baronial. The monasteries were at the height of their prosperity. Much thirteenth-century building is due to monastic patronage. If one investigates the history of some parish church which shows signs of having been much extended or rebuilt in the Early English style it will be found practically always that the church is connected with or appropriated to some monastery. Modern investigators discount the influence of the monasteries on parochial building, but it is certain that the rebuilding and extensions of many chancels were done, if not at the cost of the appropriating monastery, at least at their instigation. The austere character of the parish church at this date is most certainly to be ascribed to the influence of monasteries, just as the secular, semi-military character of the Norman churches is to be ascribed to lay patrons—soldiers and hunters.

The feudal system still held sway but was weakening ; the liberty of the individual was on a firmer footing. English law was beginning to take shape and something in the way of parliamentary government was beginning. But none of these changes are reflected in parish church building, where the supremacy of the church, and particularly the monasteries, overshadows everything. Never were churches built so entirely free from earthly motives. There was nothing to distract the soul from its heavenly pilgrimage, and the chaste detail and often elegant proportions and aspiring lines seem to direct the thoughts to higher things.

PLANNING.—The great bulk of Early English parish church building is in additions and alterations to existing fabrics, but there are plenty of small churches and a few large ones which, though a former building may have stood on the site and small portions may be incorporated, are to all intents and purposes new buildings. The plain rectangular plan, without a chancel arch, was still very commonly adopted in the Home Counties. The nave and chancel plan, with a chancel arch, was also in very general use for small buildings. Some churches seem to have been planned from the first with aisled nave and unaisled chancel—Elm is a fine example. There are a few grand examples of nave and chancel plans, aisled throughout, as Hartlepool, West Walton (4).

But the cruciform plan was still very usual in large constructions, and this is often due to monastic or cathedral influence. One of the most notable is Darlington, but the tendency is also well shown in the smaller churches of Potterne and Uffington (13, 78). Transepts are usually much longer in proportion than in twelfth-century work, and chancels are often of enormous length.

Transeptal chapels (*i.e.*, transepts opening out of the nave) began to be used very frequently. Adderbury, Oxfordshire, seems to have been so laid out from the first.

ADDITIONS AND ALTERATIONS.—The most common improvement to an existing church during this period was the lengthening of the chancel, or its rebuilding on a much larger scale. Hundreds of English chancels attained their present dimensions at this period though they may have been altered in subsequent ages ; some of them are among the noblest works of English architecture.

The custom of adding aisles to the nave still held sway. Hundreds of churches in the Midlands still retain their arcades, though the original aisles, being too low and narrow, have generally been rebuilt on a larger scale ; but in the South-eastern counties many Early English aisles, covered by an extension of the nave roof, so that the whole nave and aisles are under one gable, remain unaltered to this day (12).

Towards the middle of the thirteenth century the addition of aisles to the chancel was a marked feature in the South-eastern counties. These are generally wider and under a separate gabled roof.

Nave aisles of 1250 and later are generally much wider and were roofed with a gable, parallel to that of the nave.

The addition of transeptal chapels at the east end of the nave was very common in the South-east, the Midlands and the North.

A great many Norman churches, whether with central towers or not, seem to have had the whole of the east end newly built with central tower, transepts, and long chancel, for instance Buckland, Stanton Harcourt and Downton.

CLERESTORIES were still very rare and usually occur only in large churches, as at West Walton (4), Hartlepool, Elm, Filey (76). But some examples occur in minor churches, as at Downham ; at Hartlepool both nave and chancel possess clerestories. At Horsham, where there is no chancel arch, the thirteenth-century clerestory runs from east to west continuously.

TOWERS were still uncommon in the lesser churches except where needed for defence, a bell-cote supplying their place, but there are very many central

77 WESTWELL, KENT

78 UFFINGTON

EARLY ENGLISH INTERIORS

80   THE DETACHED BELFRY, WEST WALTON:
Early English arcading with Plate tracery

79   NORTH CERNEY, GLOUCESTERSHIRE: the
Early English Saddleback Tower

and western examples. The unsymmetrical position began to fall out of favour unless there were strong reasons for placing the tower in some eccentric position, as on the Marshland, where West Walton (80) and Sutton St. Mary and Tydd St. Giles have large detached towers some distance from the church. These are marshland churches, and the detached position is due to the desire to avoid the settlement of the heavy tower pulling down the main structure. An entirely new development in plan was the engaged western tower; the aisles continued past the tower to its west face, as at Hartlepool, Frampton, Acton.

The addition of a SPIRE to the tower is, perhaps, the most striking innovation of the Gothic style. It may have come as the logical development of the low pyramid that usually capped the Norman tower, but it was obviously in harmony with the high-pitched gable that became inevitable with the introduction of the acutely pointed arch of the lancet period in which it first appeared. The early examples are of somewhat stumpy proportions and of the broach type, rising from the outer edges of the tower walls without a parapet, both features suggesting an origin in the pyramid. Its four additional faces involved the invention of the squinch to carry them, and of the pinnacle to mask the junction and serve as a buttress.

PORCHES were still not regarded as necessities and are hardly found outside the limestone belt. They are fairly frequent in Gloucestershire, Oxfordshire and Northamptonshire; a very few are vaulted, as at Enstone, or have upper stories. Some fine examples survive with arcaded sides, as at West Walton (82), Polebrook, Warmington. The gable is generally acute, and some roofs are made entirely of stone slabs supported on transverse arches, as at Barnack. Plainer examples are usual in the Cotswolds and adjoining districts—e.g., Handborough.

WALLS AND BUTTRESSES.—Walls were generally rather thinner than in Norman work, and though the core is still of rubble they are as a whole better built. Stones in ashlar facing are generally rather longer and larger than those of the preceding periods.

Base courses are still rarely employed except where freestone was obtainable quite near; in Lincolnshire, for example, the base course is often fully developed. A simple string course is often found beneath the windows, usually of a section to throw the dripping water clear of the wall face, but a round section is very common.

The corbel table (74, 76) is rarely found except in early work, and especially beneath the eaves of towers (97)—corbelled blocks give way to moulded ones, or those of the typical mask motive. Buttresses begin to be of greater projection, but this rarely exceeds, and is often less than, the width. Very low buttresses, only reaching to the window-sills (74), and of very little practical use, are very usual and typical features of minor parish church buildings. The string courses often run round them and they may have a base even where there is no base course to the main walls ;

the weatherings are usually plain slopes. Two buttresses are usually placed at the angles; but the corner chamfering arrangements still survived. As yet the buttress did not play a very important part in the construction of the parish church. Some of the boldest are those strengthening chancels that have their walls almost completely occupied with tall lancet windows (84). In some of these the broad splays leave so little intervening wall that the support of buttresses is urgently needed, as at Cherry Hinton.

ARCHES.—The arches of the Early English period are usually constructed in rings like the Norman ones, but owing to the width of the chamfers in the plainer examples and to the rich moulding of more elaborate arches the divisions are far less marked. The arch generally in use was the pointed arch, sometimes fairly acute, but generally a good deal flatter than the equilateral proportion. Where old tradition was strong the semicircle was retained, and was often used when height was limited. The segmental arch was also employed, particularly over the rere-arches of doors.

Some elaborate doorways have arches of the pointed trefoil shape, and the same form was often applied to the heads of lancets after the middle of the thirteenth century.

SUPPORTS.—In early work the JAMBS follow the Norman formula of recesses, each with a shaft, but the shafts are often detached, and in later work these stand clear; the recesses may be hollowed out, and the Norman formula is developed into an arrangement very free, giving the effect of a shafted splay instead of a series of recesses.

PIERS.—Detached supports in small churches and in many large ones are generally circular, but the octagon was gaining in favour (85). The clustered types, originated in the Transitional period (86), continued to be used in larger churches, but they are much less common than the plain circular column. A few churches have piers with detached shafts, as at West Walton (4). In the West some piers are characterised by groups of triple shafts, usually under the influence of Wells Cathedral.

WINDOWS.—The tall, narrow window of this period, with its pointed arch, is unmistakable. So tall and narrow are most of them that the usually accepted name, lancet, is not inapt.

Usually they were intended for glass, and the glass here is very near the outer wall face, the interior being very widely splayed. Lancet windows are usually of severe simplicity and externally they have but a chamfer or a chamfer and recess. The heads of small lancets may be in one stone, but they are more often in two. An external hood mould is common (13, 87) but is often omitted (75). Very rarely the jambs may be moulded, and in very exceptional examples there are shafts in the jambs, and these may have moulded or foliaged capitals (84). There is generally a string course under the sill (75).

Internally the splay is usually quite plain, but in more elaborate churches there may be a moulded rere-arch, with or without shafts in the jambs (83).

81 THE WEST DOORWAY   82 THE SOUTH PORCH

THE LUXURIANT MARSHLAND EARLY ENGLISH OF WEST WALTON

84 THE EAST END, WESTON, LINCOLNSHIRE:
a typical Early English composition

83 THE PREBENDAL CHAPEL, THAME, OXFORD-
SHIRE: developed Early English window design

86   THE NORTH ARCADE, WEST

85   THE SOUTH ARCADE, EAST

CONTRASTS IN PIER DESIGN, EATON BRAY

87 THE NORTH NAVE ARCADE, EATON BRAY, BEDFORDSHIRE,
with characteristic Early English carving and arch mouldings

Windows are often grouped in pairs (74) or triplets (13, 84), and examples of five and even seven grouped lancets occur. In these windows the wide internal splays meet and a common shaft serves to support the rere-arch of two adjacent lancets. In this case a triple or quadruple shaft sometimes occurs.

When the lancets are not quite so close the rere-arches may be linked in a continuous arcade, as at Cherry Hinton.

Some of the most beautiful compositions may be found at the east end of chancels or the ends of transepts (13, 84).

DOORWAYS.—The extraordinary elaboration of the doorways of Norman date, which had begun to pass away in the Transition period, was practically discontinued in the thirteenth century except in the finer and more important churches. Many little churches have the plainest possible doorways of one order, chamfered, sometimes with a moulded impost, and usually with a hood mould. Some are of two orders, generally chamfered, but sometimes the outer ring of the arch is moulded with more or less elaboration, and the jambs have shafts, usually standing clear of the recesses. Often the capitals are foliaged, but more frequently they are moulded only. Doorways with arches in more than two orders are not common, but when they occur they are often chastely beautiful (81, 89). It became very usual to mould the angle of each recess or even to treat it as a secondary shaft. The only really common enrichment of the arch moulds is the dog-tooth (82, 89), but in a few early examples a sort of chevron, boldly detached and therefore commonly broken off, is employed with good effect. Foliage is only used in the mouldings of a few very rich doorways. The rere-arch is usually quite plain, but may have a hood mould. It is usually segmental in shape and not so much stilted above the main arch as in Norman work.

CARVING.—Probably there is no period of English architecture when carving was so sparingly used, but when it is introduced it is practically always of masterly technique, even in small churches. In more important buildings the foliaged caps, in their feeling of life and growth, are perhaps the nearest to perfection of all capitals of any period.

The foliage is usually fronded, or a trefoil with rounded lobes springing from a stiff strong stem, which gradually emerges from the bell of the capital, the foliage breaking clear and twisting and curling most engagingly (92). In early examples the stem is more important than the foliage, but the tendency was for the foliage to grow at the expense of the stem. The latest examples are marvellously undercut (93, 94), and it is often impossible to believe that these clusters of foliage, so full of life, once lay within a round cylinder of stone.

Grotesque animals and birds are sometimes introduced, as at Burgh next Aylsham, and, in very late work, human heads, as at Woodstock.

Apart from capitals, foliage is rarely used, except in little balls to terminate hood moulds or string courses, and in spandrels. It is unusual to find foliage enriching a hollow moulding, as at Warmington; as already noted, the usual motive for continuous ornament in mouldings is the dog-tooth—a series of little pyramids, the base notched to produce petals—a motive very widely spread and subject to little variation in parish church work.

Figure sculpture is very rarely employed in architectural carving at this period.

ROOFS.—There are many roofs which, in spite of later repairs, retain their original thirteenth-century form. All were gabled, except high-pitched lean-to roofs over aisles, and flat roofs were never used.

The traditional braced rafter roof has often survived, sometimes with tie-beams at intervals bearing king-posts, treated as little columns with capitals and bases, supporting a longitudinal beam or purlin under the collars of the rafters. Theoretically this method of construction, which is extremely picturesque, should prevent any spreading of the rafters.

In the West of England the braces were worked to give an arched outline to each pair of rafters, a type of roof which was highly developed even at this date in Devon. A roof at Berrynarbor was decorated with fine foliaged bosses.

Rough tie-beam roofs were no doubt used, of the sort which still persisted in seventeenth-century barns. A rather more elaborate example at Little Coxwell may fall within this period, in which the openings of the ties are cusped.

Apart from mouldings to tie-beams and cornice-plates and king-posts, Early English roofs are extremely plain. As yet the notion of treating them decoratively had not been conceived.

Warmington, Northamptonshire, about 1260, is one of the first instances of the use of flat roofs covered with lead, and here the actual roof is concealed with wooden vaulting, as if the carpenters felt themselves unequal to the task of making such a roof a thing of beauty.

SUMMING UP.—Early English work is most common in the South-eastern counties, including Essex, but the best is found in the limestone districts and the North-east. It is very rare in the South-west, Lancashire and Cheshire and uncommon in East Anglia.

The style is extraordinarily austere, and the vast majority of churches of this date are practically devoid of all carved detail: even mouldings are very sparingly used; any beauty they possess is due to fine proportion. The reaction against the superabundant ornament of some Norman work is very striking. Really elaborate Early English detail is frequent in the district around the Wash (81, 82, 94), and is very uncommon elsewhere.

When all the resources of the style are employed—detached shafts, foliaged capitals and rich mouldings—the effect is chaste and dignified, but

89 MUMBY, LINCOLNSHIRE

88 FARNDISH, NORTHAMPTONSHIRE

EARLY ENGLISH DOORWAYS

EARLY ENGLISH CAPITALS

always very restrained, very ecclesiastical, often a little aloof and impersonal, academic (4, 87).

As compared with Norman fabrics the Early English churches are better built, more elegant in their proportions, and better lighted, except those which had the characteristic low lean-to aisles which are even gloomier than those of the preceding century, as at Grosmont and Bury, Sussex (12). They had a great advantage in the greater length and dignity of their chancels and in the more ample provision for side altars in aisles, transepts, transeptal chapels and choir aisles.

Norman represents the perfection of centuries of Romanesque building. Early English is the first phase of the Gothic, and as such is experimental, immature. It had jettisoned the marvellous decorative resources of the Normans and in its place could only offer stiff-leafed foliage and the dog-tooth, and even these were sparingly used. Plain moulded capitals (90) are far more often found than foliaged ones. The standard of achievement, so remarkably uniform in the Norman period, fluctuated very much in the Early English style. The lancet window is certainly a beautiful thing, but a church lighted entirely with lancets has a monotony of effect. Later builders realised this and corrected it by improved forms of window.

The greatest achievements in the style are the long unaisled chancels, such as Cherry Hinton, Stanton Harcourt, Adwalton, and certain arcades, such as those of Ivinghoe, Eaton Bray (87), St. Mary le Wigford, All Saints, Stamford, and, above all, of West Walton (4). Some east ends, such as Ockham, Blakeney, Polebrook, also reach a wonderfully high standard. But on the whole it may be said that the best brains and energy were at work on the cathedral and abbey churches, and that only a small pro- portion of parochial building is of the first class.

At this point it may be well to consider how far the Early English parish church was an improvement over its predecessor.

The chancels of the period are obviously a great advance on those of Norman churches, more spacious, better lighted, often of magnificent proportions, and of lovely chaste detail, admirably fitted for the celebration of High Mass and the singing of the Hours. The transepts, also, are equally well lighted, and often provide room for more altars. But the nave, because of the addition of aisles, was even more gloomy than before, owing to the very general absence of a clerestory and the dependence on the light from little lancets low down in the side walls. It is rarely that a church remains in this condition, but when it does it is easy to appreciate why later builders would not rest content with the work of their forefathers. Such naves as Grosmont are extraordinarily dark, and the great high-pitched gable covering both nave and aisles (12) has a picturesque but barn-like effect. The aisles are much too narrow to make really good side chapels. They are practically only useful as procession-ways. Yet this was the type of church which prevailed in parish after parish. Not one in seventy-five had a clerestory, and without it the nave could not be adequately lighted nor the beauty of the arcades properly appreciated. Churches with clerestories, such as West Walton (4), Hartlepool, Darlington—even lesser examples, such as West Tarring or Horsham—came very much nearer to perfection, and in these cases there is some cause to regret the later alterations. As a rule, however, there was ample cause for the insertion of larger windows, the raising and widening of the aisles and the addition of a clerestory.

92 EATON BRAY

93 SLIMBRIDGE, GLOUCESTERSHIRE

94 WEST WALTON, NORTH CHANCEL ARCH PIER
EARLY ENGLISH FOLIATED CAPITALS

96 OXFORDSHIRE PINNACLED TYPE, WITNEY

95 THRECKINGHAM, LINCOLNSHIRE

CHAPTER IX

THE TRANSITION FROM EARLY ENGLISH TO DECORATED

In the middle of the thirteenth century there was a distinct reaction against the growth of monastic influence, which culminated in the Statute of Mortmain which, in theory if not entirely in effect, checked the granting of further land to the Church, and practically stopped the foundation of new abbeys on a large scale. The result was that benefactors devoted their attention to the parish church. Those who wished to provide for the welfare of their souls had to be content with the foundation of a chantry at some parish church.

The period is also marked by the rise of lesser county gentry. The power of the great feudal overlords was waning and the sub-tenant was in a more independent position.

The chivalric ideal of society was coming into fashion, with its handmaid heraldry, and the architecture of the period reflects these changes and takes on a less austere aspect.

The great change of the period was the evolution of the mullioned and traceried window, a change due to the ever-present desire for more light, rendered feasible by the greater cheapness of glass. The effect was to broaden all the proportions. Good work was also done in the development of spire design.

It was a period of church enlargement rather than of reconstruction. Churches entirely of geometrical style are extremely rare. Cotterstock is an example of nave and chancel and west tower plan, while Mowsley, Leicestershire, shows a nave and chancel with transeptal chapels on both sides. Bishop Auckland (98) is a larger building but is mostly of earlier origin. The plan shows long chancel, aisled nave and transeptal chapels with west tower. Warmington retains older arcades, but the long chancel and the wide aisles and west tower are of this period. This is one of the oldest instances of the use of flat roofs to the clerestoried nave and aisles.

Two of the most important enterprises of the period are the remodelling of two central tower churches by the addition of very wide gabled aisles—Grantham and Great Yarmouth. At the former a west tower was built, two bays west of the older church, flanked by huge aisles, which were eventually, but much later, extended to the extreme end of the chancel. At Yarmouth the aisles were much wider than the nave, and were brought out flush with the end walls of the older transepts of the cruciform church.

But geometrical work is usually found in small portions of a building, frequently in the addition or widening of aisles to nave (11) or chancel, the addition of transeptal chapels or the extension of chancels. The cruciform plan with central tower about this time went completely out of fashion.

The period is also notable for the growing use of west towers of a purely religious nature—campanili, not fortresses—and the beginning of the popularity of spires.

ARCHES AND SUPPORTS.—The arch stones may be chamfered or moulded. If moulded, the mouldings generally lie on a quadrant surface and the junction of their rings is worked into a deep hollow. The hood mould generally has human heads for stops.

Pillars are generally circular or octagonal, or they may be clustered, usually of more or less circular outline or plan.

The water-holding base gives place to a series of three flat rounds.

The capitals (98) are very rarely carved. In the rare cases where carving occurs it has a tendency towards naturalistic forms, and the stem of the leaves is less accentuated. Sometimes the general outline is more convex than concave. In most examples the capitals are moulded, usually rather elaborately, with a multitude of tiny members, the scroll being popular.

DOORWAYS.—These are rare, and difficult to assign to their proper period. Plain examples are simply chamfered (99), and may sometimes be distinguished by the use of human heads as stops to the hood mould, which may be of the scroll form (118), so called from its resemblance, in section, to a roll of parchment.

Elaborate doors of the period are very uncommon. The jambs are shafted, the Norman motive of a series of rectangular recesses being hardly recognisable owing to the moulding and the shafts of the intervening angles. The capitals are invariably round, rarely foliaged, and if so, in rather a naturalistic manner; if moulded, with many very fine members in which the scroll mould is pretty sure to appear, usually on the abacus.

The moulding of the arch, though still built in orders, does not clearly reveal the original square form of the arch stones, the members generally being arranged on a quadrant surface to fit well on the round capitals. The usual plain face at the point between the rings is often removed, forming a deep circular hollow. Dog-tooth is sometimes used and may be of very elaborate design, but other enrichment is extremely rare in parochial work.

WINDOWS.—The great achievement of the period is the introduction of the traceried window of two or more lights.

Tracery was not invented; it gradually evolved, tentatively and experimentally, over a period of three hundred years or more.

The pre-Conquest builders had employed openings of two lights, separated by balusters or shafts—for instance at Brixworth, over the west door (2), or in the belfry windows of many towers (42, 55). In a little group of towers in the North they had gone so far as to frame the whole

97 HALLATON, LEICESTERSHIRE: an early English broach Spire of Midland
type with the beginnings of tracery

98 BISHOP'S AUCKLAND, CO. DURHAM, showing the transition from Early English to Decorated

99 EWYAS HAROLD

100 ACONBURY

HEREFORDSHIRE TRACERY BEGINNINGS

101 RYTON CHANCEL,
CO. DURHAM

102 NORTH KILWORTH,
LEICESTERSHIRE

103 SOUTH SIDE OF RIPPLE CHANCEL, WORCESTERSHIRE

EXPERIMENTS TOWARDS TRACERY FROM THE LANCET FORM

composition with a pilaster strip, bent round in semicircular shape, and to pierce a little circular opening in the spandrel or "tympanum" between the arched lights and the surrounding frame.

Though the Normans refrained from using two-light openings in the outer walls of nave or chancel, they often used them in belfry lights, using their favourite formula of the arch in two rings. The first went round the small openings, the second enclosed the whole composition, as at Brayton (55). A similar treatment was employed in the design of the triforium of a great church, and here again the space between the small arches and the great containing arch was relieved by piercings of geometrical form.

The Early English builders continued to use a similar arrangement in belfries (79) and triforia, the tendency through all being to increase the size and number of the piercings.

In the body of the church it became the fashion to group lancets in pairs or triplets (83, 84), bringing them ever closer and closer until the rere-arches shared a common shaft. Still they were wide apart externally. When they were brought still closer together the wide internal splays ran into each other and could no longer support the internal arch. For a while a detached shaft performed this office, but the step of bridging the internal opening with a single arch was inevitable. Thence it was a small step to show the internal arrangement outside, by framing the group of lancets in a single-arched hood mould.

Often a circular window above a group of smaller openings had been employed in Norman façades. The opening tended to be placed in closer and closer conjunction with the lancets. Finally it was placed between the lancets and the hood mould (99, 100, 103).

Then it was realised that the tall gables of the great thirteenth-century churches afforded the suitable space for a large window of many lights. The openings in the spandrel were increased in size and number (100, 103). Then the spaces between the geometrical figures were pierced and the result was complete geometrical tracery, formed by moulded bars of similar section (105). It was a revolutionary invention. No longer need the churches be gloomy and ill-lighted. The church could be almost entirely of windows stretching from buttress to buttress; but as the window was increased in size, so the wall was weakened and needed buttresses of bolder projection to stiffen it (103). Henceforward the demand was always for more window, more stained glass, lighter and lighter construction.

It is interesting to trace the ancestry of geometrical designs. There are those descended from two lancets with a diamond opening above (102), or a circle (105), or a vesica, and those whose origin may be traced to the favourite group of three lancets, the centre the tallest (103).

But the old tradition of narrow single lancets died very hard, especially in the West Midlands. The Romanesque fashion of separating the openings or lights by shafts with caps and bases also died very hard.

Many geometrical windows have very fully developed shafts set against the moulded mullions (105). The device is common in later work all through the fourteenth century, if funds were plentiful, as at Heckington (117). The shafts tended to get smaller and smaller, and were less and less often used, though they survived in Devonshire work of the late fifteenth and early sixteenth centuries.

Cusping.—The idea of foliating an arch is of very early origin. Many Norman doors have the outline of their first ring worked into a trefoil shape, as at Nately, Bibury, Clymping (41). At Condover the circular window in the gable has a quatrefoil opening. Similar windows occur in the clerestories of Bourne and Newton, of late twelfth-century date.

Oddly enough, the idea of foliating the head of a window does not seem to have followed directly. Probably it was first employed in the rere-arch, as at Cherry Hinton, and was then transferred to the window opening.

At Barfreston (39) and Castle Hedingham the large circular windows of the gables were partly filled in by a radiating arcade which can only be described as tracery. The device was probably derived from triforium openings, but may have been imported from Italy, though this is unlikely, for our native masons liked to worry out a new invention step by step without borrowing from the foreigner.

Many small churches of the third and last quarters of the thirteenth century contented themselves with cusping the lancets of the side walls, reserving the traceried window for the east end. A late example of this conservatism is the chancel of Stanton St. John, Oxfordshire, where the small cusped lancets of the side walls are obviously of the same workmanship as the fully developed three-light Decorated east window.

106 NORTHORPE CHANCEL,
LINCOLNSHIRE

105 WEST WALTON

SIMPLE FORMS OF GEOMETRICAL TRACERY

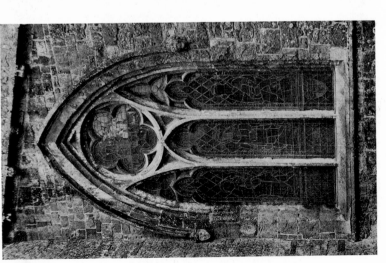

104 MIDDLETON CHENEY,
NORTHAMPTONSHIRE

107 ETCHINGHAM, SUSSEX

108 CHINNOR, OXFORDSHIRE

DECORATED VILLAGE CHURCHES

CHAPTER X

THE DECORATED STYLE

INTRODUCTION.—Towards the end of the thirteenth century church architecture took on a more general and human aspect, freed from the austerity of monasticism and also from the tyranny of the compasses. All the details are pervaded by the changing curve of double curvature known as the ogee.

The prevailing influence of the time was chivalry. Wealth was becoming much more evenly distributed. The patrons of the Church were very often the lesser gentry and small landholders, and those who had acquired wealth as soldiers of fortune. The wool trade was enormously increasing the wealth of the country, and this and the introduction of the weaving industry produced a class of wealthy commoners who were anxious to follow the example of the aristocracy in the founding and building of chantry chapels at their parish churches. It was an age of chantry chapel building, and these usually took the form of aisles to the chancel, transeptal chapels, or the addition or widening of the nave aisles. Very often the effigies of the founders remain in their arched recesses near the altars of these chapels, or at least the tomb recesses remain.

Trade was not the only way of amassing wealth; a feature of the time is the number of churchmen—often lawyers—holding high offices of State, who were rewarded with wealthy livings, often held in plurality, and situated in widely separated parts of the country.

The monastic ideal of austerity was falling altogether into the background. The pomp of chivalry, the joy of battle, the pride of life, the love of beauty and refinement, were much more important matters. Life was beginning to be a more pleasant affair. The feudal system with its hardships for the poor was losing much of its rigour. The wages of labourers were increasing, and landowners found it more and more difficult to enforce the feudal rights to the labour of their tenants.

The successful wars of Edward I. with Scotland, and the conquest of Wales, followed by the successes of the English army in France in Edward III.'s reign, aroused a feeling of national pride and patriotism.

The architecture of the period is full of gay beauty, the work of men who found this life very pleasant. Its forms are suave and gracious, its proportions comely, its carved details full of humour and the love of nature.

The sweetly smiling human faces of the hood-mould stops (121), compared with the scowling, semi-architectural masks of the thirteenth

K

century or the grotesque monsters of the twelfth, give the keynote of the period.

PLANNING.—Owing to the growing prosperity of the country a greater number of churches were entirely rebuilt, but in most instances it is clear that the plan is affected by the original layout. Patrington, Snettisham (115) and Shottesbrooke, for example, retain their cruciform plan, though they were completely rebuilt in the style of the period, when the west end was preferred for the tower, and transepts were not in favour.

Little rectangular churches continued to be built, especially in outlying hamlets. The nave and chancel plan also continued, with the chancel almost or quite as wide as the nave, and the chancel arch very wide. In Norfolk and Suffolk many churches were built on this plan but with enormously wide naves, as at Elsing. The usual method here seems to have been to build new side walls outside the older and narrower nave, and much higher, so that the new nave could be completed before the older building was removed, but in some cases, where an older western tower remains, quite out of centre with the nave, as at Blundeston, the widening must have taken place on one side only.

It was a great period of aisle-widening and heightening. Hundreds of the narrow lean-to aisles of Norman or Early English date were swept away to give place to the newer fashion of wide and lofty aisles. So in hundreds of churches throughout the land Early English arches are found leading into Decorated aisles. Where the former aisle was of decent width the walls were heightened to give room for taller windows, and the roof flattened, for lead seems to have been coming into general use except in the South of England.

Transeptal chapels, as in the magnificent church of Heckington (117), were still very popular and sometimes of great length, accommodating at least two altars in each. At Witney the long Early English transepts, already planned for two altars, were lengthened to provide yet another altar. Aisles added to the chancel are fairly frequent at this period, particularly in the South-east, though Beverley St. Mary and Holy Trinity, Hull, are fine northern examples.

Large chapels flanking the chancel were also built, e.g., Shifnal, and many smaller instances in Kent.

The period is also celebrated for its magnificent unaisled chancels, such as Hawton, masterpieces of English craftsmanship, while many smaller churches had their chancels extended, or at least the east window remodelled in the new style.

Everywhere the little Norman slits and narrow Early English lancets gave place to the larger windows of this style, letting in a flood of light.

In East Anglia and Lincolnshire, especially, the prosperity of the new weaving industry led to the complete rebuilding of church after church, usually with unaisled chancel, aisled nave and western tower. The only

109 CHARTHAM, KENT, with Kentish tracery

110 ST. BOTOLPH'S, BOSTON, LINCOLNSHIRE: the Nave and South Porch

111 HOLY TRINITY, HULL, LOOKING EASTWARD. A lofty late Decorated arcade, showing the transition to Perpendicular in the east window and arch mouldings

112 PEMBRIDGE, HEREFORDSHIRE

113 GREAT MISSENDEN, BUCKINGHAMSHIRE

DECORATED VILLAGE INTERIORS

115   SNETTISHAM, NORFOLK.   Unusual central Tower plan

114   WHISSENDINE, RUTLAND

VILLAGE CHURCHES OF THE DECORATED PERIOD

relic of the former church may be the dimensions of the nave, the old foundations being usually employed as a base for the pillars of the arcade.

The cruciform plan waned in popularity. The liturgical movement of the twelfth and thirteenth centuries had lost its force and there was no longer a desire to turn the parish church into a little cathedral. The performances of all the liturgical offices was regarded as secondary to the multiplication of Masses at the ever-increasing number of side altars. Very few, if any, churches were built now with central towers, though the former existence of this fine feature often led to its retention in the new style. Patrington (5) is one of the finest cruciform churches ever built. But already there was a tendency to pull down the central tower and build a new one at the west end.

CLERESTORIES began to be common in some parts of the country. They are most usual in Northamptonshire—following the example of Warmington—but soon spread to Lincolnshire and East Anglia, and the South Midland counties (108). As a rule they were very low, with circular openings, but in Northamptonshire, Rutland and Lincolnshire they are often of considerable height with large two-light windows. At Boston (110) two of these are used in each bay. In Norfolk the openings are generally circular, exceptionally large, and in some cases they are alternated with two-light arched windows.

Flat roofs began to be general over naves and aisles, and these led to the general use of parapets, hitherto almost unknown in parish churches—giving them an altogether different aspect—but the fashion did not spread to the West until later.

TOWERS were built in large numbers, particularly in East Anglia. In Northamptonshire and Lincolnshire, Rutland and Lancashire, these frequently had magnificent spires. Many Early English towers had Decorated spires added, notably Stamford St. Mary and Ketton. The development of spire design and its spread from Northamptonshire north and south along the limestone belt is a feature of the period. Some of these are among the finest achievements of the English race, such as Heckington, Ewerby, Bloxham.

The period is marked by the constructional improvement of the spire by slanting it from the inner instead of the outer face of the tower wall, and by surrounding it with a parapet. Pinnacles were often built in the four angles to weight them and give them power to resist the thrust of the spire (115), leading to great picturesqueness of outline.

PORCHES began to be regarded as a necessity even for the smallest churches. Where stone was scarce, clumsy wooden structures were built; where it was plentiful the porch was of stone, often with an upper story, reached by a winding stair in an octagonal turret. But as yet the treatment was restrained (116). It was for the next age to make the porch one of the loveliest features of the church.

WALLS.—The walling of this period is generally much better built than ever before. The ashlar is in large blocks, well squared and perfectly jointed. Rubble work is often squared and coursed, if the nature of the stone allowed. In flint districts the walls are generally faced with split flints to give a more even surface (127).

The base course is rarely absent and was very fully developed in Lincolnshire (117, 118), where it is often of considerable height and bold projection; but where stone was scarce it was still omitted or took the form of a simple chamfered offset. In more important churches there is generally a string course below the window-sills, usually of very simple section (108, 130).

There is often a moulded cornice to the walls, even when there is no parapet. Parapets first became general at this period. Generally they are low, with a deep moulded course and coping. Battlemented parapets came into very general use in the counties round Northamptonshire, but are rare elsewhere. The parapet is occasionally decorated with sunk tracery, and in late examples is sometimes of open tracery work, but this is very rare indeed. St. Mary Magdalene, Oxford, is a fine example.

Buttresses (117, 118) were made with very much greater projection than heretofore, because, in spite of the absence of stone vaults, the wall, seriously weakened by the large windows, needed stiffening. As yet there is little attempt at any systematic planning of buttresses in relation to the bays of the arcade, except in East Anglia, where its advantage was appreciated much earlier than elsewhere.

Decorated buttresses usually rise to the eaves (116) and in Lincolnshire often extend to stiffen the parapet. The offsets are usually plain chamfers, but the top is often gabled and the lower offsets often have a gable (117), sometimes combined with the usual slope. A niche is often found in the face of a buttress and some of these are of charming and delicate detail (118). They were always intended to contain figures of saints.

At this period a single diagonal buttress was often used at the angles instead of a pair placed square with the building, but both methods were employed.

Often the angles of a gable-end were reinforced with pinnacles of large size (116), a device particularly common in the chancels of East Anglian churches.

In some of the more important churches of the end of the period smaller pinnacles rise from the buttresses and tower above the parapet, as at Boston (110) or Sandiacre.

ARCHES AND SUPPORTS.—The ARCADES were generally taller and more graceful in proportion than those of preceding eras, especially in East Anglia and Lincolnshire; elsewhere the proportions are more stocky.

The ARCHES are rarely moulded with any elaboration. Still built in two rings, the arch stones may be chamfered, but are often wave-moulded,

117   THE SOUTH TRANSEPT, HECKINGTON

DECORATED DESIGN, PLAIN AND RICH

116   THE SOUTH PORCH, PATRINGTON

118 THE SOUTH PORCH, HECKINGTON, LINCOLNSHIRE. Decorated
work of full-flowered luxuriance

119, 120   PATRINGTON NAVE

121   THE VESTRY, HAWTON, NOTTINGHAMSHIRE

DECORATED CAPITALS

THE DECORATED DOORWAY

or ovolo-moulded. The recess between the two rings is often worked into a deep hollow.

The circular PIER was generally discontinued. Smaller churches of the date have octagonal piers (112). A group of four circular shafts (111) is common, and these often have a fillet worked on the cardinal faces. Sometimes the shafts are of marked ogee plan. The four shafts may be separated by a deep hollow (111), or somewhat illogically (since it supports nothing) by a little shaft. Clusters of eight more or less equal shafts are found in some large churches, but arranged in a diamond plan instead of a circle.

Very often the capital is omitted and the mouldings of the arch arise from the floor without any break.

CAPITALS are practically always circular and moulded, but the octagon plan for the cap came in in the second quarter of the fourteenth century. Foliaged caps are very rare, but when they occur they are extremely beautiful. They are less uncommon in the North-east than elsewhere (119, 120). Usually the foliage is natural or flowery, very closely packed, giving a bulbous outline to the capital (121). In North Oxfordshire several churches have capitals composed of human busts with interlinked arms, as at Bloxham and Hanwell. Those at Ludgershall, Buckinghamshire, are especially good.

DOORWAYS.—It is curious to observe how entirely attention had been directed at this period from the doorway to the window.

Most Decorated doorways are extremely plain. Probably the most common is an arch in two rings, both wave-moulded, the section continued down to the floor without a break (123). The hood mould is pretty sure to be a scroll and tiny roll, terminated by heads of knight and lady or king and queen. In rather more elaborate examples the recess between the rings may be hollowed out, and a similar hollow may occur between the hood and the arch. On another type the mouldings of jamb and arch are different and intersect at the springing, without the use of capitals or bases.

Some elaborate doorways have shafts to the jambs, but the general lay of the mouldings and shafts is a splay, not a series of recesses (122). Some doorways have the hood mould and sometimes the arch itself of the lovely ogee shape, sometimes crocketed (124). Enrichments are not often used in the mouldings, but the characteristic ball flower is sometimes employed (122), or little square flowers of bulbous modelling sometimes connected by a running stem. A very few have continuous trails of beautiful foliage, at first naturalistic, and latterly of the bulbous type. The arches of a few doorways are beautifully cusped and foliated, as at Cley.

WINDOWS.—The beauty of the windows and tracery is the greatest joy of this style. The variety of design is positively amazing. Windows of one, two, three—up to seven—lights are found in parish churches, and though the favourite arch is the equilateral, it may be lower or higher than this. Segmental, pointed segmental, ogee and square arches were also employed if the case demanded some abnormal treatment.

In small churches, and particularly in early work, the tracery was brought forward to the wall face, but in most cases it was set in, not as a rule more than five inches, and the tracery was framed in a moulded surround. The shadow thus produced and the variation in the planes of window and wall are of the greatest artistic value.

Internally there was usually a rere-arch, springing generally from a lower level and not rising above the apex of the window tracery. Shafts are sometimes used in the jambs, particularly in Lincolnshire (129), but not very often elsewhere. Generally the tendency was to simplify the internal frame of the window more and more.

The tracery formed the centering for the construction of the outer arch. A wood centre was required for the rere-arch. The intervening space was usually bridged over with long stones, giving a winding surface which was generally plastered.

The marvellous variety of Decorated tracery design has been analysed, pigeon-holed and docketed by E. A. Freeman (*Window Tracery*, 1851), but nothing is to be gained by such ultra-scientific methods, though one might note one or two of the main types :—

1. Grouped lancets.—This was one of the first motives, and continued for some time.
2. Intersecting.—From every mullion spring two arched mullions of the same radius as the containing arch, intersecting with one another and forming in the head a series of four-sided figures.
3. Reticulated.—The tracery consists of a number of similar geometrical forms—trefoils or quatrefoils of the same width as the lights below, each tier diminishing in number (14, 130), *vide* p. 77.
4. Flowing (126-130).

A large window was usually laid out as a series of windows linked together by the containing arch. The principle is known as sub-arcuation, and tended to give the design system and unity. We may note how the notion of a central circle survived well into the flowing period (127), as at Chipping Norton, as a filling for the spandrel between the sub-arches and main arch. Circular windows were not in common use, but charming examples occur at Cheltenham, Leek, Staffordshire, and on a smaller scale in porches at Hunstanton and Gooderstone.

ROOFS.—The art of the carpenter began to develop at this period. Though the old braced rafter roof remained very much in favour, the double-framed roof became more usual, and for a good reason. The large windows of the style seriously weakened the walls. It was advisable to concentrate weight and thrust on the piers between the openings, and this was the great advantage of the double-framed roof with principals and

127 AYLSHAM SOUTH TRANSEPT,
NORFOLK

126 WEST END OF SOUTH AISLE,
HEDON, YORKSHIRE

CURVILINEAR TRACERY DESIGN

125 THE FLEMISH CHAPEL, BEVERLEY
ST. MARY, YORKSHIRE

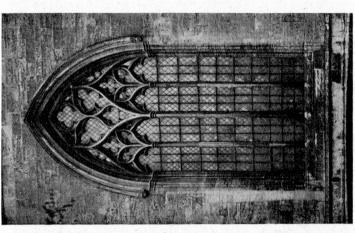

128 GRANTHAM, LINCOLNSHIRE

129 SLEAFORD, LINCOLNSHIRE

130 THE RETICULATED EAST WIN-
DOW, MADLEY, HEREFORDSHIRE

THE GRACE OF CURVILINEAR WINDOW TRACERY

132   ADDERBURY NAVE, OXFORDSHIRE

DECORATED ROOFS

131   DENNINGTON NAVE, SUFFOLK

133 DETAIL OF THE SEDILIA CANOPIES, HAWTON: the full
Elaboration of Decorated Detail

purlins. Many of the roofs of this period are of fairly flat pitch and covered with lead, and these were constructed by using beams for the principals, choosing timbers that were naturally cambered, and if necessary adding other beams on the top to produce an obtusely gabled form. The purlins lay directly on the beam, or were raised as necessary to suit the required pitch on blocks or posts. To prevent the beam from sagging, arched braces framed into wall posts were often added.

For roofs of medium pitch the gable was formed by principal rafters, leaned on to the beam at the lower end and pitching against a king-post at the head ; braces were often added and these were cut into cusps, making the principal into a great piece of tracery. Fine roofs of this sort remain at Adderbury (132) and Stanton Harcourt. A typical example of a lean-to roof of the date is seen at Mendlesham, where the purlins are carried on posts arising out of a tie-beam.

Usually a Decorated roof is very plain and massive (131), and each principal differs from the other according to the natural bend of the oak tree.

There are some roofs of the arch-braced form which may be as early as the first half of the fourteenth century, such as Malton, where the construction is rendered more rigid by wind braces, set against the under side of the rafters and rising from the principal rafters to the purlins. A fine example of the arch-braced type of roof from East Anglia is that of the chancel of Tunsted. As in all mediæval roofs except those with tie-beams, the principal must be considered as a wooden arch, and that is very rightly the lines on which it has been designed.

SUMMING UP.—As a result of the operations of the Decorated builders the average standard of parish church architecture was vastly improved. Even if only a few traceried windows were inserted the result was to brighten the interior and give to the exterior a piquant effect of contrast. Where more important works were carried out the improvement was vast. No longer was the church a dimly lit barn ; the large windows of the spacious aisles lent a good deal of their light to the nave, showing up the beauties of Norman or Transitional arcades or the crisp foliage of Early English capitals. And if some Early English chancels had their symmetry destroyed by the insertion of great Decorated windows here and there, the result was to give the structure a kind of life. Where a clerestory was undertaken, the improvement of the top lighting was inestimable.

When the Decorated master craftsmen had done their work the church was altogether more attractive, more human, less aloof and austere. Our churches owe very much to the work of this wonderful period. If we compare the churches of Sussex with those of South Lincolnshire and Northamptonshire, we get an idea of what the fourteenth century did for the thirteenth.

CHAPTER XI

THE TRANSITION FROM DECORATED TO PERPENDICULAR

THE last and the longest in duration of the mediæval styles was not marked by any revolutionary invention such as the pointed arch or the window of many lights; its special contribution to construction, the four-centred arch, is by no means an essential feature of the style, though it is a very beautiful and useful device. It was rather the development of the former style into a perfect and logical system.

It is by no means easy to describe the transition from Decorated to Perpendicular. It differs from the former transitions in that it was no gradual and widespread change of fashion immediately accepted in all districts. The new style appeared almost perfectly developed in the cathedral church of Gloucester as early as 1337, but the innovations there employed did not meet with general acceptance except in the immediate vicinity. In some districts, such as East Anglia, the Decorated style continued to be employed down to the very end of the fourteenth century, with only minor though very beautiful variations of detail and proportion. Yet the development of Perpendicular by a slow process of evolution went on in districts where the new tracery forms of the Gloucester masons were probably unknown.

The most striking characteristics of the later Gothic work are the general lightening of the structure; the logical correlation of each part to the other; the reduction of the piers to the lightest possible proportions (6, 111); the more or less complete suppression of wall surface, due to the increased width of the windows, and the greater projection of the buttresses combined with a reduction in the breadth.

Most of these tendencies are first seen in the churches of the friars, which were buildings of moderate cost, rarely if ever vaulted, and therefore more akin to parochial than monastic building, intended mainly as large auditoria for the preaching which played so large a part in the work of the friars. It is hardly possible to exaggerate the influence of the friars' churches on the general structure and proportions of the later parish churches.

On the other hand, the general tendency of the period to minuteness and delicacy in the details of moulding and carving may be traced to the influence of the tomb maker and minor craft workers, who began to come into prominence at the end of the thirteenth century; many characteristics

76

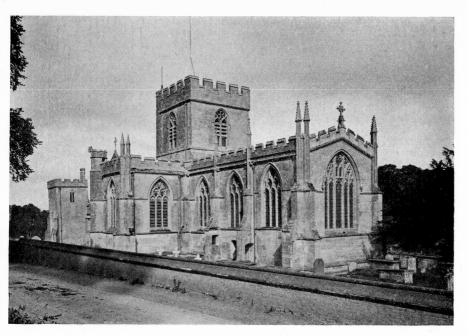

FROM THE SOUTH-EAST

FROM THE WEST

134 A NOTABLE EARLY PERPENDICULAR CHURCH, EDINGTON, WILTSHIRE

135 SUTTON, CAMBRIDGESHIRE

136 WIGGENHALL ST MARY THE VIRGIN, NORFOLK

EARLY PERPENDICULAR CHURCHES IN EAST ANGLIA

137   THE EAST WINDOW, FISHLAKE.   138   THE EAST WINDOW, WELWICK
THE TRANSITION TO PERPENDICULAR IN YORKSHIRE WINDOW TRACERY

139 THE WEST FRONT, BEVERLEY ST. MARY: a vigorous
Perpendicular remodelling of an earlier church

of the later Gothic style occur very early in the tombs, Easter sepulchres, sedilia and other stone fittings which they produced. These features are the first to show the vertical elongation of proportion, the slimming of buttresses, shafts and pinnacles, the reduction in scale of individual members of the moulding, and the greater minuteness of carved details. These were beginning to assume great importance in the church interior. In contrast to these delicate works of art, the bolder features and mouldings of an earlier age often look coarse and out of scale, and it was natural to bring the structure into line with its contents.

As regards the new development of tracery in which vertical lines predominate, exactly balanced over those of the lights or mullions below, though this is peculiar to England and Wales, it is the logical and inevitable outcome of tracery design, and the gradual transition is perfectly easy to trace. Delightful as the Decorated windows of geometrical or curvilinear design usually are, it must be recognised that the tracery often has too little relation to the supporting mullions. One might go so far as to say that the most completely satisfying are those in which the design of the tracery is set out to correspond with the lights below, as, for instance, in the most common type of all—the reticulated (108, 130).* These are more restful and dignified than the freer designs, because there is a unity between the lower and the upper parts of the window which appealed strongly to the later Gothic masons, who carried the principle still further by introducing vertical lines into the tracery to bring it still more closely into harmony with the verticality of the mullions. Though the shapes left by the tracery mullions are less varied and interesting in themselves they lend themselves much more readily to the art of the stained-glass painter, who could put a saint into each little panel, and this in itself was sufficient to ensure the general adoption of Perpendicular design, for stained glass was reaching a much more pleasing and more popular stage of development. The greater proportion of white glass had not only the virtue of admitting more light, but also that of allowing scenes and figures to be represented in a less conventional manner. And also the employment of more white and less coloured glass made picture windows cheaper, for the white was a home production, while coloured glass was usually imported.

The growth in popularity and output of the craft of stained glass is largely responsible for the greater size of the windows in the later churches, and this led naturally to the necessity for a more logical distribution of the parts of a building. It was necessary to increase the proportional projection

---

* As a design for a two-light window this unit of tracery is obviously appropriate and beautiful, and its popularity may account for its repetition in larger windows on the Greek principle of " give us a good thing twice or thrice." Some readers, however, may feel that Ruskin's denunciation of Perpendicular tracery as monotonous and lacking in design might be more justly applied to the repetition of a single unit in windows of this type, particularly as the enclosing arch usually cuts the outer edges of the pattern so abruptly as to produce fragments of awkward and uncouth shapes.

of the buttresses to ensure the safety of the weakened walls, and also to contrive piers and roof principals so that they corresponded with the dimensions of the outer walls.

The four-centred arch was a development from the pointed segmental arch used in the thirteenth and fourteenth centuries when the height was limited. The angular intersection between jambs and arch was unpleasant to the later builders who quite naturally and inevitably rounded off the awkward angle.

By means of the four-centred arch it is possible to span any opening, however limited the height, still retaining the point at the apex and avoiding any harsh angularity. It is also peculiarly logical. The lower courses of a pointed arch are merely corbelling. It is natural enough to mark the distinction between the stones of the arch which are actually an extension of the support and those which form the arch proper by a change of curve.

The four-centred arch never entirely displaced the two-centred arch. It is employed in some of the earliest Perpendicular work, and its flatness or acuteness is no criterion of date.

There are very few entire churches which show Transition-Decorated-Perpendicular throughout. Edington in Wiltshire (134) and Sutton in the Isle of Ely (135) are outstanding examples, and these show a singular admixture of Decorated forms with the newer ideas. It is more usual to find Decorated and Perpendicular forms side by side in the same building, and in this case it is often very difficult to decide whether the features are actually contemporary or not. The chancels of Boston and Patrington are instances, and Nantwich.

The Transition in tracery (111, 127, 138) is well represented in windows in the Midlands, as in the east window of Charlton on Otmoor, the north aisles of Hampton Poyle and South Newington, and the south aisles of Great Rollright and Merton.

In Norfolk (136) the Transition is marked by the retention of Decorated details in mouldings and tracery, in buildings which otherwise have the light and airy proportions of the later style.

It is rare to find Transition-Decorated-Perpendicular features in the North or the South of England or in the extreme West. Undoubtedly the phase originated in the West Midlands.

140 SOUTHWOLD, SUFFOLK: a stately Perpendicular East Anglian church of
flint flushwork

141   CROWCOMBE, WEST SOMERSET: a Perpendicular village church
with plain Tower and no clerestory

142 MINSTER LOVELL ON THE EDGE OF THE COTSWOLDS, OXFORD-
SHIRE: rebuilt on the original cruciform plan

143 KINGSTON ON THE QUANTOCKS, SOMERSET
PERPENDICULAR VILLAGE CHURCHES

144 ASHBURTON, DEVONSHIRE

145 LAVENHAM, SUFFOLK

GREAT PERPENDICULAR CHURCHES OF SMALL TOWNS, EAST AND WEST

CHAPTER XII

THE PERPENDICULAR STYLE

HISTORICAL INTRODUCTION.—In the fourteenth century the wool trade was the basis of England's prosperity; even foreign policy was dictated by this paramount industry. The merchant was at least as great a man as the soldier, and was beginning to rival the great landholder as a patron of the arts. This tendency was still more marked in the fifteenth century, when the aristocracy was impoverished by the long Wars of the Roses, even if its members escaped the fate of being killed in battle or executed afterwards. The wealth of the country came more and more into the hands of commoners, and it was to a great extent by commoners that the Perpendicular churches were built. The rebuilding of Lavenham Church (145), for example, begun by a great noble, De Vere, Earl of Oxford, was completed by a great merchant, Spring.

The Black Death of 1349 reduced the numbers of the population to an enormous degree, and labour became scarce and wages high. Even small traders and farmers in their new freedom could contribute liberally towards the cost of building. Many churches were built by the subscriptions of the parish, and lists of subscribers have survived, for example, among the churchwardens' accounts at Thame.

The finest churches of the period are to be found where the wool trade and the weaving industry were most prosperous—in East Anglia (139, 146), the Cotswolds (6, 154), Somerset (143, 180), and Devon (144, 160).

The disastrous war in France and the long drawn-out struggle of the Roses had astonishingly little effect on the normal life of the period, but the former had the result of cutting this country off from free communication with the head-waters of Gothic Art—the Ile de France. English architecture had become more and more insular since the middle of the thirteenth century, and tended to become more and more separated from Continental influences. Until the days of Henry VIII. and the introduction of French and Italian artists in the Renaissance style, English architecture pursued its own way without foreign inspiration.

The same thing was happening all over Europe. Each country was developing its Gothic art on separate and individual lines. It is interesting to note that the latest phase of Gothic architecture in France, the beautiful Flamboyant style, was developed from elements evolved in England during the fourteenth century at the very period when we were developing from the same elements the entirely different, yet equally logical, Perpendicular.

79

With the growth of individual liberty and the more even distribution of wealth, parish life was very strong; it was centred in the parish church. Religion since the Black Death and its attendant horrors had taken a very personal and somewhat mystical turn, very much overshadowed by the thought of death and judgment. New cults of Aspects of the Passion and of the saints arose. Every one wished to make provision for the welfare of his soul. Those who could afford to endow chantries were fewer, but it was possible by forming a guild to share in the Masses which it maintained. So guilds became more and more a factor in church architecture. Each guild must have its altar, and if there was no room for another, a chapel must be built for it. Whether these guilds were primarily trade associations or entirely religious mattered little. Religion dominated English life. The farmers or the butchers of a town considered a chapel of their own as essential as did the Guild of the Holy Cross.

The liturgical movement, with its orderly following of the old customs in imitation of those in use in all the cathedrals, was even more than before in the background. The parish services were largely a multiplication of Low Masses, and local devotion and extra liturgical anthems in honour of local saints were considered of equal importance with the Canonical Hours.

Perpendicular architecture, then, shows none of the austerity of monasticism, nor is it instinct with the pride of chivalry. It is more practical and common-sense, but this does not mean that it is dull. We have more fine buildings of the Perpendicular style than of all the other styles together. The wealthy commoner of the fifteenth century was at least as good a churchman as his aristocratic predecessors, and the buildings he paid for are undoubtedly the best that have been evolved from the point of view of the ordinary parishioner.

At the moment it would seem that the Perpendicular style, instead of coming gradually, was, without any definite idea of creating a new style, originated by an individual, the master mason, whose name is lost, of the south transept of Gloucester Cathedral, to meet the needs of a particular case. The problem was the transformation of the gloomy and massive Norman work at the smallest possible cost into a more graceful and comely form. More light was called for and a vast area for the display of stained glass, which was becoming one of the ruling passions of the day. His solution was to hide the older building by a screen of fine stone, treating each bay of the structure as a huge window from floor to vault. In a sort of reaction against the ponderous Norman style he carried almost to excess the lightness of his new screen work. The tall mullions needed lateral support, which he obtained by further transoms at frequent intervals. Thus he secured not merely a larger window with stronger resistance to wind pressure, but also a large series of panels of varying and graduated sizes, each of a rectangular form suitable for the reception of a picture in stained glass.

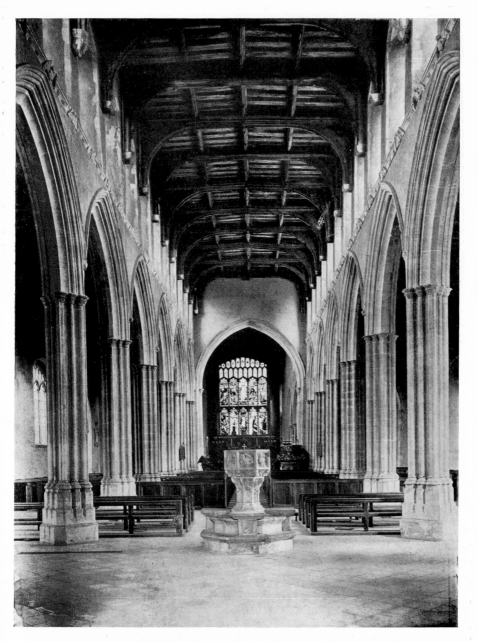

146 STOKE BY NAYLAND, SUFFOLK

147 OLD RADNOR : RADNORSHIRE. A typical Perpendicular interior

The necessities of the planning of a late Gothic church were primarily a great nave for preaching, wide aisles for processions and a multitude of chapels for the altars of guilds or chantries. The chancel, as a rule, mattered less, and is often mean compared with the rest of the fabric.

PLANNING.—The growth of the local pride of a village or town is manifest in the building of innumerable towers and spires and in porches large and small, every one a gem of architecture.

Since money was more plentiful the Perpendicular builders were often able, and, like their Norman predecessors, usually inclined, to sweep away an earlier building, or at least everything west of the chancel arch, and rebuild on a new plan. They were thus able to reconcile the conflicting demands for a great auditorium and for a congeries of chantry chapels, for these could be provided, not as separate buildings but by screening off bays of the wide aisles or even the spaces between the piers of the arcades.

More frequently, however, such a clean sweep was not possible, and the founders of chantries had to be content with widening an existing aisle or enlarging an earlier chapel.

WALLS.—Mason-craft had improved enormously. Walls are usually of moderate thickness and in the freestone districts often faced within and without with ashlar. But little wall was left between the enormous windows, which sometimes stretch from buttress to buttress—especially in clerestories the wall is practically a continuous series of windows—almost entirely in wrought stone (17, 19, 140). Ashlar is commonly in large blocks and finely jointed. Often there is a certain admixture of bricks ; in stoneless districts brick is much more common (159, 171).

Base courses are usual, though in the West they may be omitted. Often in Norfolk and Suffolk they were fully developed and richly decorated with sunk tracery (170) or flint inlay ; the joints between the split flints are often " galleted," i.e., small chips of flint are pressed into the mortar. Bases are higher than ever before, except in Lincolnshire in the fourteenth century. Often the thickness of the wall is reduced under the windows, forming a sort of seat in the low sill ; or this reduction may be achieved by panelling the surface. Perhaps the majority of the walls of this date are crowned with parapets (168-172) and a large proportion embattled (144, 145). The string course below the parapet is generally marked by a deep and wide hollow, flanked by splayed fillets and weathered above. It is often enriched with carved gargoyles, frequently of considerable projection, usually in the form of monsters (168, 169). The parapet is frequently enriched with sunk tracery (169).

WINDOWS.—To read the accounts of Perpendicular tracery in the handbooks, one would imagine that a window of this period was a monstrosity devoid of every grace. The straight mullions, we are told, always run up to the head, and similar lines run up from the head of each light. Then sundry horizontal lines, called transoms, divide the whole into a series of rectangular panels, each of which is treated in a precisely similar way, with an arched and cusped head. What a picture! And how rarely, except in immature work at Gloucester or Worcester, do we find anything of the sort!

Granted that the suave flowing lines of the later Decorated are more graceful, yet the introduction of the vertical line is artistically valuable in echoing the vertical lines of the buttresses, the horizontal in reflecting those of base course and parapet, making the window an integral part of the building instead of an insertion.

The Perpendicular tracery is the logical outcome of the reticulated pattern. Though the mullions do not usually run straight up to the head, the design of the tracery is balanced out over the spacing of the lights below, two lights in the head to each main light; thus there is a unity between the main part of the window and its tracery. Each tracery light is of a convenient shape to receive a stained-glass figure.

The variety of Perpendicular windows is almost equal to that of Decorated (96, 139, 148). Every district has its favourite patterns. Compare, for instance, East Anglia at Southwold (140), Kersey (154), and Cavendish (150), with Somerset at Crowcombe (141) and Devon at Ashburton (144) and the North (139, 149).

The arches in use were usually more obtuse, though very acute ones occur when the case demanded it, as at Bloxham. Segmental (145), pointed segmental (139) and square heads (151) often occur, but the special arch of the period is the four-centred (148), a most beautiful and flexible form, accommodating itself to every contingency. It can be made very flat, the lower curves of small radius, the upper very large, or, by increasing the radius of the lower arch, it can be made acute, as acute, in fact, as one struck from two centres but of a more subtle and pleasant shape.

Except in East Anglia, where the scarcity of stone forbade it, the tracery was generally set well back from the wall face, casting a lovely shadow on the head of the arch. In sandstone districts especially it was usually set in the centre of the wall. The main lines of the design were in mullions of large section, the lesser being carefully graduated in thickness according to their length.

DOORWAYS AND PORCHES.—The doorways were usually delicately moulded, the members lying on a chamfer plane, divided into two groups by a deep and rather wide hollow, known as a casement. Generally the jambs continue the same moulding as that of the arch, but often the jamb has one or more slender shafts with octagonal moulded capital and base, supporting ogee members in the arch. In East Anglia the chamfer plane is less rigidly adhered to, and the shafts are often bolder. There is also less uniformity in the scale of the various members.

The arch is very frequently of four-centred outline, but the two-centred arch, of rather obtuse shape, was almost as popular.

149   THE EAST END OF THE SOUTH AISLE,
        BRANT BROUGHTON, LINCOLNSHIRE

PERPENDICULAR TRACERY

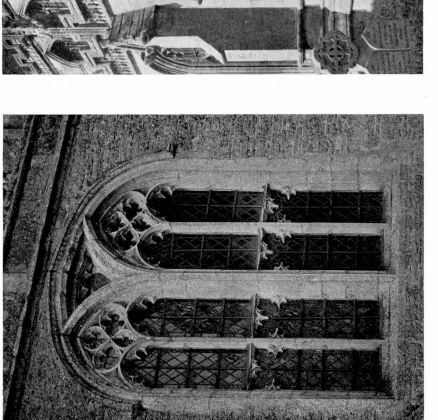

148   THE SOUTH TRANSEPT, LOWICK,
        NORTHAMPTONSHIRE

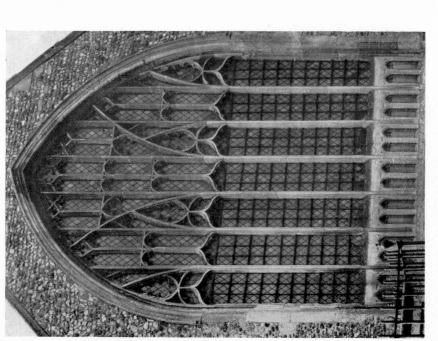

151　THE SOUTH AISLE, CLIFTON REYNES,
BUCKINGHAMSHIRE

150　THE EAST WINDOW, CAVENDISH,
SUFFOLK

THE VARIETY OF PERPENDICULAR TRACERY

153   THE SOUTH PORCH, KERSEY, SUFFOLK:
in flint flushwork

EAST ANGLIAN PERPENDICULAR PORCH DESIGN

152   THE SOUTH PORCH, CLEY, NORFOLK

154 THE SOUTH PORCH OF NORTHLEACH, GLOUCESTERSHIRE:
a Cotswold " Wool " church

The most characteristic feature of a Perpendicular doorway is the framing of the arch in a rectangle (8, 152, 158). Sometimes only the hood mould takes the rectangular outline, but often the outer group of mouldings also helps to form the rectangular frame. The spandrels afford a good opportunity for relief carving—either tracery, heraldry, or foliage, but often figure subjects. Less common but far more graceful is the ogee hood mould, usually crisply crocketed. Northleach has a fine example. Doorways treated in this manner are frequently flanked by attached buttresses and pinnacles.

It was not unusual in richer examples to carve a niche for a figure in the hollow mouldings of the jambs.

The ogee and the square frame are sometimes combined in the same composition.

Undoubtedly the churches of the limestone belt and those of East Anglia can show the best examples ; elsewhere the fifteenth-century doorway is of less interest.

The luxury of a porch to protect the main entrance of the church had always been the ambition of the parishes that could afford it. The church door was a place where much mediæval business was done ; bargains and contracts, for example, were confirmed there, and, since marriage was in part a contract, the wedding ceremony began there. New notions of comfort and convenience, seen in the domestic buildings of the age, now caused the porch to be regarded as more than a mere luxury. Where there was none the omission was supplied, and often, when the existing porch was small, it was rebuilt on a larger scale. Many churches were given porches on both north and south, and some, like King's Sutton, at the west as well.

These were often built with an upper story so as to provide a room which may have been used by the sacristan or by the priest who slept in it, so as to be up in time to celebrate an early Mass for travellers, but which was probably also the school in which a chantry priest taught the choir boys as one of the conditions of the endowment by which he lived. This use of the room, as we learn from many allusions in contemporary literature, persisted long after the Reformation. Shakespeare speaks of " a pedant that keeps a school in a church." Aubrey tells that both he and Hobbes went to school in the church porch at Malmesbury, and there are wills of schoolmasters who desire to be buried in the church—" at the foot of the stair that goeth up to my schole." A fireplace is therefore a very usual fitting to the upper chamber, and its chimney always illustrates the artistry with which the mediæval builder " turned his necessity to glorious gain," and made a useful thing a thing of beauty. The porch at Northleach (154) had candle sconces over the fireplace, and in the priest's room at Warmington, Warwickshire, there is even a latrine contrived in one of the buttresses.

The porch also enabled the builders to gratify another ambition of the mediæval architect and crown his work with a stone vault. The problems of providing adequate abutment, so that his vault should be stable and without danger to the rest of the fabric, were easily solved in the case of the porch ; and so here the vault is in many districts the rule rather than the exception, and is often a gem of the lovely fan-tracery which was the Perpendicular architect's great contribution to the solution of the age-old problem of vault construction (160, 161).

CARVING.—As compared with that of the preceding style, carving became less florid and sumptuous and more clear-cut and restrained, and usually more delicate in scale.

Foliage is rarely employed in capitals, except in Devon and the adjoining parts of Somerset, where a convex and usually continuous band of foliage occupied the whole space between the abacus and necking (165, 166). The standard of merit varies, but some Perpendicular foliage vies with the best carving of the Decorated period in freedom of invention and boldness of cutting.

In Somerset and Wiltshire a slight decoration of the capitals with leaves of diamond outline is not uncommon. Elsewhere foliage capitals are extremely rare (162), though there are instances in East Anglia, the foliage being very small in scale and of geometrical outline.

String courses were often enriched with flowing foliage of more or less naturalistic design, generally founded on the vine or oak, or with square bosses at regular intervals (155).

Spandrels were very often decorated with foliage, generally highly conventionalised.

External string courses below parapets were generally relieved by gargoyles, often grotesque monsters with bat-like wings, more rarely human caricatures.

Figure sculpture was less freely employed in minor carvings and was less graceful and picturesque in character, and indeed less competently handled, though much of the spandrel carving of East Anglian doorways is delightful, showing considerable skill in its adaptation to the awkward space available.

Perhaps the roof corbels are the most usual positions to find figure carvings. Human heads are very frequently employed, especially in the Cotswolds ; and as the fashions of the day were very faithfully represented these often afford useful clues to the date. Undoubtedly these heads are less skilfully cut and more conventional in treatment than those of the Decorated period.

Angels were a favourite motive with the carvers of the fifteenth century (167, 173, 174, 177). Usually in the upper half the angel is represented rising from a band of conventional clouds, and holds a shield or scroll or other emblem. The standard of merit varied considerably. Some are exceedingly crude, but there is a good proportion of very competent and

155 THE INNER PORCH-ARCH, ST. MARY THE GREAT, CAMBRIDGE

156 THE WEST DOORWAY, MAIDS
MORETON, BUCKINGHAM

157 THE VESTRY DOORWAY, HILLES-
DEN, BUCKINGHAMSHIRE

PERPENDICULAR DOORWAYS

159 RAYLEIGH, ESSEX : craftsmanship in brick

158 LAUNCESTON, CORNWALL : elaboration in granite

PORCH DESIGN IN UNUSUAL MATERIALS

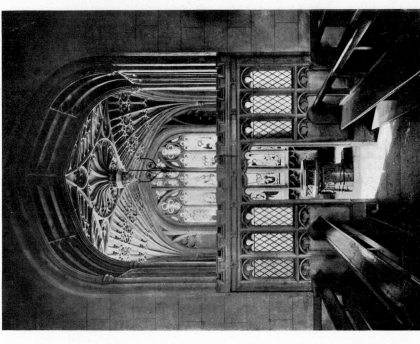

161 THE BAPTISTERY, ST. LAURENCE, EVESHAM,
WORCESTERSHIRE

160 THE SOUTH AISLE, CULLOMPTON, DEVON

PAROCHIAL FAN VAULTING

164 NAVE CAPITAL, CLIFTON REYNES,
BUCKINGHAMSHIRE

163 NAVE PIER-BASE, BLOXHAM,
OXFORDSHIRE

THE PERPENDICULAR CAPITAL AND BASE

162 THE NAVE, MOLD,
FLINTSHIRE

165 THE SOUTH ARCADE, TIMBERSCOMBE, SOMERSET

166 SWYMBRIDGE, DEVON

167 REWE, DEVON

WEST COUNTRY PERPENDICULAR FOLIATED AND FIGURE CAPITALS

168 FONTMELL MAGNA, DORSET

169 THE TOWER, WENTLOOGE, MONMOUTHSHIRE

170 BASE COURSE OF THE TOWER, HOXNE, SUFFOLK

PERPENDICULAR PARAPETS, ETC.

171 THE CLERESTORY, GREAT BADDOW, ESSEX

172 BATCOMBE, SOMERSET

173 THE DOUBLE HAMMERBEAM NAVE ROOF, SWAFFHAM, NORFOLK

delightful work, especially in the Cotswolds and East Anglia. But the carver was now dominated by architectural requirements and was allowed less liberty.

Roofs.—Towards the end of the fourteenth century the craft of the carpenter came into its own ; in fact the master carpenter was as important a craftsman as the master mason. In many parts of England the churches would be dull if it were not for the fine construction of their Perpendicular roofs. Often the roof is far more decorative and richly ornamented than any other part of the church. And that is as it should be. The principle of increasing the richness and delicacy of the work as the building rises is a very sound one. Flat roofs of the cambered-beam and firred-beam type are common all over the Midlands, and are treated with exceptional richness in Cheshire and Somerset, the type also occurring in Lancashire, Dorset, Yorkshire and Shropshire. In these districts the beams and purlins are richly moulded and often increased in number till the roof surface consists of a series of square, deeply moulded panels (147). Sometimes each panel is transomed and almost always the intersections of the tie-beams are decorated with carved bosses. A trail of tracery often decorates the beams and purlins in the North-west Midlands.

In Somerset the tie-beam roof of moderate pitch, usually lead-covered, was treated similarly, the openings of the principals filled in with tracery (177). A simpler form of the tie-beam roof, with hammer-beam principals between each tie-beam principal, is typical of the Marshland district. It is odd that roof design falls off very badly in Lincolnshire. In Yorkshire arch braces are commonly inserted beneath the beams of tie-beam roofs and the effect is a little depressing, as at Hull or Almondbury.

In Kent, Sussex, Surrey and Hampshire the old braced rafter roofs with their king-posts and tie-beams were continued, flat roofs being uncommon.

Devon, Cornwall and Somerset also retained the old braced rafter roofs, in a double form, having principals and purlins but with each pair of rafters braced, giving the effect of a skeleton barrel vault. When boarded over and decorated with cross-ribs and casing as at Cullompton the effect was magnificent (176).

But East Anglia has the finest roofs of the period. In addition to the Marshland type already discussed, there was the arch-braced, the hammer-beam (174) and the double hammer-beam (173) roof, all moulded with great delicacy. Generally they were of very moderate pitch, the size of the timbers by no means massive, and no attempt whatever was made to counteract the thrust. The principals were regarded as wooden arches and constructed accordingly, but their thrust was brought down as low as possible by elongating the wall posts (173). The lavish use of angels on roof decoration is particularly characteristic of East Anglia at this period.

Hammer-beam roofs of a different nature are a feature of the Denbighshire churches, where, as in most of Mid and North Wales, a very massive version of the arch-braced roof was much in favour.

TOWERS AND SPIRES.—The quality that differentiates architecture from mere building is due to an intuition of the architect that his work is a monument as well as the solution of a practical problem. It was this feeling that caused the Normans to sweep away the otherwise soundly constructed churches of the conquered race, and this is mainly responsible for the existence of the tower and wholly for the spire.

Perpendicular towers, especially, are far larger and loftier than is needed merely to house the bells and give them necessary elevation. Sometimes, indeed, the tower added or rebuilt in the fifteenth century is so imposing as to spoil the proportions of the church by dwarfing the rest of the building.

It is sometimes objected that "horizontal" would have been as appropriate as "perpendicular" to describe the culminating phase of Gothic; the impression made by a fifteenth-century tower should be sufficient to dispel this illusion. The principle of verticality is everywhere manifest—in the pinnacles, which are more numerous and loftier than in the previous styles; in the windows, where the flexibility of the four-centred arch is used to advantage in acutely pointed forms, and most of all, perhaps, in the buttresses, which by their numerous offsets give the impression of upward progress to the pinnacles by which they are crowned. In some of the finer towers they are set, not as elsewhere in the building, diagonally at the corners, but in pairs as in the Early English period; not, however, in contact, but set a little back from the angle so that the quoins of the tower are seen between them, running upwards in one long vertical line and emphasising the height (179).

A tower so built hardly needs a spire, and indeed spires are perhaps less common in the Perpendicular than in the previous style. They are, however, almost invariably superior to any of earlier date, better proportioned, more elegant, and, most important of all, more harmonious in design with the towers from which they spring (11).

SUMMING UP.—When architectural criticism became a cult, in the Victorian age, it fell into the hands of amateurs of whom Ruskin was the most eloquent, and, perhaps, the most consistently perverse. With little technical knowledge and no practical experience they awarded praise or blame on abstract principles formulated by themselves. They propounded a theory that Gothic architecture reached its meridian in the year 1300 and then slowly but steadily declined for the next two centuries, after which it lingered in a debased form until the advent of Inigo Jones and Wren.

The truth is, of course, that Gothic was progressive to the last and was never more alive and vigorous than when church-building came to a sudden halt at the Reformation. The aims of its creators throughout its whole course had been to achieve greater stability at less cost of material, to improve lighting, and to reduce the risks of fire by ceiling the structure

174   THE NAVE, CAWSTON, NORFOLK

175   THE NAVE, ATTLEBOROUGH, NORFOLK

EAST ANGLIAN ROOF DESIGN

177 LONG SUTTON, SOMERSET

WEST COUNTRY PERPENDICULAR ROOF TYPES

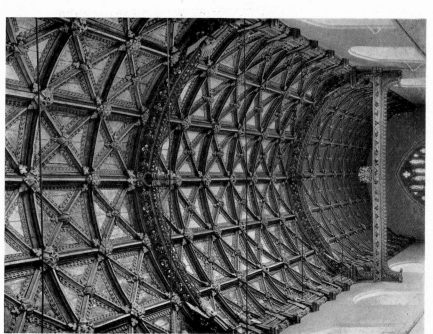

176 CULLOMPTON, DEVON

179　BRADNINCH, DEVON

178　PETERSTOW, HEREFORDSHIRE

PERPENDICULAR TOWER DESIGN

180 ISLE ABBOTS, SOMERSET

with a stone vault. These objects were completely achieved only in the Perpendicular period. It was only then that Gothic arrived at its logical conclusion and a church became a great stone lantern, its roofs stably poised, its arch-thrusts reduced to a minimum, all concentrated at a few points scientifically buttressed, or perfectly balanced one against another.

Perpendicular differed from the earlier styles, of course, as Early English, say, differed from Norman; but the essential difference in both cases was that the later produced, for a given quantity of material, a more stable building and was therefore a superior system. Perpendicular lacked some of the austere dignity of Early English as Early English lacked the massive grandeur of Norman. It lacked, too, the obvious variety in its carving, which led the Victorians to imagine that the earlier workmen were free artists, at full liberty to express themselves in their tasks. No ordinary workmen, masons and labourers, were ever so free; they had, as always, to carry out the designs of the masters of their craft. And even the carvers, who were but a small proportion of those engaged upon the building, must have worked as they had been taught to do, according to an established technique, and were probably no more and no less free to indulge their own fancies, if they had any, in Early English than in Perpendicular times. The variety in a Perpendicular building must be looked for by the trained eye, not in the ornamental but in the constructive detail, in the varying thickness of the mullions, for example, according to their length and the strain upon them, or in the varying height of the arches according to their position—wide and low in an aisle window or a clerestory, narrow and high in the upper stories of a tower.

The ignorant contempt of the Victorian amateur for Perpendicular was a new and passing phase. The eighteenth-century architects knew better, and when, as they often did, they tried their hands at Gothic, it was at Perpendicular that they essayed. When Sir William Lee, for example, rebuilt Hartwell Church, Buckinghamshire, in 1756, he, or his architect, took the fifteenth-century Chapter House of York as his model, and when Thomas Prowse, the contemporary squire of Wicken, in the neighbouring county of Northampton, rebuilt his parish church a year or two later, he also adopted a version of Perpendicular.

It was left to the nineteenth century to sing the praises of the embryo at the expense of the developed organism and to forget that the end crowns the work.

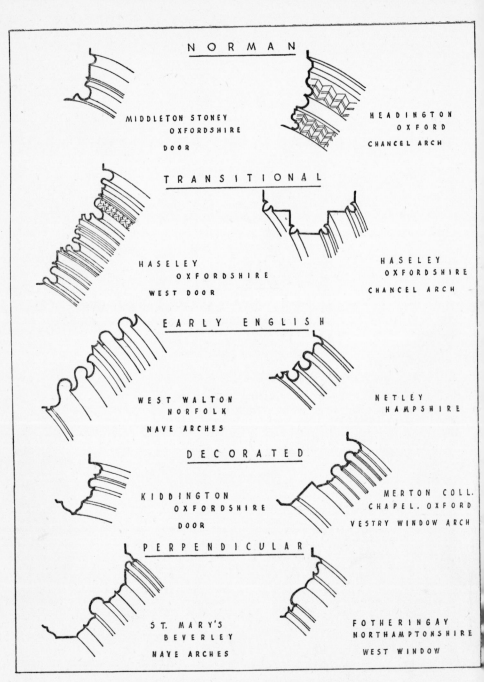

THE MOULDINGS OF THE SUCCESSIVE STYLES.

BRIEF GLOSSARY OF ARCHITECTURAL TERMS

ABACUS.—The uppermost member of a capital from which an arch springs.

APSE.—A semicircular or polygonal east end to a church.

ARCADE.—A range of arches supported by columns or piers, either open or " blind," *i.e.*, closed with masonry. Arcading was often used as wall-strengthening decoration. (*See* WALL ARCADE.)

BALL-FLOWER.—An enrichment resembling a ball in a circular flower, and carved in a hollow moulding. Characteristic ornament of Decorated work.

BALUSTER.—In Anglo-Saxon work a short " turned " stone column used in window openings, particularly in the belfry story.

BARREL VAULT.—A roof covering of either stone or brick, of semicircular section.

BASE COURSE.—A strengthening course at the foot of exterior walls. From a simple chamfered form it developed to considerable height and mouldings of bold projection.

BAYS.—The compartments into which the nave or roof of a building are divided by columns, buttresses, or roof principals.

BILLET.—A Norman enrichment consisting of short cylinders or square pieces, usually in a hollow moulding.

CHANTRY CHAPEL.—A chapel within or attached to a church, endowed for the saying of Masses for the soul of the testator or others.

CLERESTORY.—The side wall of a church above the aisle roof and nave arcade, usually pierced with windows.

CORBEL.—A block, usually moulded or carved, projecting from a wall and supporting a superincumbent weight.

CORBEL TABLE.—A connected range of corbels immediately beneath the eaves of a building ; it can also support a parapet.

CROCKETS.—Decorative features occurring principally at the angles of canopies, pinnacles, and spires ; generally carved and placed equidistantly.

CUSHION CAP.—A Norman capital in which the lower part of the block of stone forming the capital is made round to fit the column and the upper part square to fit the abacus.

CUSPS.—In tracery the small pointed members which intersect the foils, or small arc openings, and constitute foliation in the form of trefoils, quatrefoils, etc.

DOG-TOOTH ORNAMENT.—An Early English ornament of small four-leaf pyramids, usually set in a hollow moulding and repeated either continuously or at short intervals.

GROINED VAULT.—A vault formed by the intersection of two barrel vaults at right angles, the groins being the " arrises " or lines of intersection which cross the area diagonally.

HAMMERBEAM ROOF.—A wooden roof in which the tie-beam is dispensed with and its place taken by projecting beams ; the ends of these are generally treated decoratively. A second range of tiers makes a DOUBLE HAMMERBEAM ROOF.

HOOD MOULD.—A projecting moulding, designed to throw off rain, around the arch of a window, doorway, or archway. Also known as Label or Dripstone.

IMPOST.—A horizontal projecting member from which an arch springs.

JAMBS.—The upright sides of doorway and window openings.

LANCET WINDOW.—A name applied to the narrow-pointed window of Early English Gothic from its resemblance to a lancet blade.

MULLIONS.—The vertical divisions between lights in a Gothic window, from which the tracery springs.

NARTHEX.—A single-story porch across the end of a Roman basilica and found in a few pre-Conquest churches.

OGEE.—A compound curve, partly convex and partly concave ; the term is applied to sections of mouldings and outlines of arches.

PIER.—A supporting member from which arches and vaulting spring, in form usually rectangular, polygonal, or clustered, and composed of a collection of shafts and mouldings.

PILASTER STRIPS.—In Saxon work, narrow vertical strips of stone of slight projection, decorating exterior walls and forming patterns with connecting diagonal and arch-shaped stones.

PISCINA.—A shallow stone basin, with a drain, set in a niche south of an altar for washing sacred vessels.

QUOINS.—The wrought stones at the angles or corners of buildings.

RERE-ARCH.—The inner arch which supports the wall over the recess of a window or door as distinct from the outer arch.

RESPOND.—A half pillar or corbelled termination to an arcade.

ROOD LOFT.—A gallery over the rood screen, or chancel screen, originally supporting the rood or crucifix.

SEDILIA.—Recessed seats for priests on the south side of the chancel, generally of masonry and canopied.

SHAFT.—A small column, either independent or a member of a clustered pier. (*See* PIER.)

SPANDREL.—The triangular space formed between two arches, or between one arch and the lines of a rectangular hood mould.

STRING COURSE.—A projecting horizontal band or moulding on a wall, often continued round a building.

TRACERY.—The ornamental stonework in the heads of Gothic windows, springing from and supported by the mullions. Circular windows were also filled with tracery. The earliest form, " Plate " tracery, consists of circles and other geometrical figures cut in solid stonework. After the middle of the thirteenth century the tracery was built up of stone bars and known as " Bar " tracery.

TRANSOMS.—The horizontal bars in windows.

TRIFORIUM.—The story above the arcade enclosed by the roof of a side aisle. In cathedrals and large churches it is often a vaulted gallery between the arcade and the clerestory.

TYMPANUM.—The space enclosed between the lintel and the arch in Norman and Gothic buildings, often filled with sculpture or ornament.

VOLUTE.—A spiral ornament, characteristic of the classic Ionic capital and sometimes found in Norman capitals.

VOUSSOIRS.—The wedge-shaped stones or bricks which form an arch.

WALL ARCADE.—A blank, or " blind," arcade used as a form of wall strengthening or decoration.

BRIEF INDEX OF ILLUSTRATIONS AND CHIEF TEXT REFERENCES, ARRANGED UNDER COUNTIES

NOTE.—*References in heavier type are to the* FIGURE NUMBERS *of Illustrations.*

ENGLAND

BEDFORDSHIRE

Eaton Bray, 63, **85, 86, 87, 92**   Farndish, **88**

BERKSHIRE

Faringdon, 54, **67, 72**   Uffington, **13, 14,** 58, **78**
Little Faringdon, **70, 74**

BUCKINGHAMSHIRE

Clifton Reynes, **151, 164**   Hillesden, **157**
Fingest, **40**   Maids Moreton, **156**
Great Missenden, **113**   Wing, 21, **23,** 26, 31, 32
Hartwell, 87

CAMBRIDGESHIRE

Cambridge St. Mary the Great, **155**   Soham, **65**
Cherry Hinton, 60, 61, 63, 68   Sutton, Isle of Ely, 78, **135**

CORNWALL

Launceston, **158**   Perranzabuloe, 25
Madron, 25   St. Gwithian, 25
Morwenstow, 14

DERBYSHIRE

Melbourne, 40, **46**   Steetley, 37
Repton, 25, 26, 28, **31,** 31, 33

DEVON

Ashburton, 82, **144**   Rewe, **167**
Berrynarbor, 62   Swymbridge, **166**
Bradninch, **179**   Torquay, Tor Hill, 25
Cullompton, 85, **160, 176**

92

DORSET

Fontmell Magna, **168**

Studland, **37**

DURHAM

Bishop Auckland, 65, **98**
Durham, 31, 56
Easington, **52**
Escomb, **20**, 21

Hartlepool, 58, 64
Monkwearmouth, 21, 22, 25, 27, 29, 31
Ryton, **101**

ESSEX

Bradwell-on-Sea, 19, 20, 22
Castle Hedingham, 46, 54, 68
Great Baddow, **171**

Greenstead, 18
Langford, 26, 31, 32
Rayleigh, **159**

GLOUCESTERSHIRE

Bibury, 10, 27, 29, 68
Bishop's Cleeve, **9**, 13, 40, 55
Brimpsfield, 14, 47
Cirencester, **6**
Deerhurst, 26, **30**, 30
Elkstone, 47, 49, **60**

Gloucester Cathedral, 76, 80
Hampnet, 42, 47
North Cerney, **79**
Northleach, 83, **154**
Slimbridge, **93**
Windrush, **61**

HAMPSHIRE

Silchester, 17, 20, 22

HEREFORDSHIRE

Aconbury, **100**
Brayton, **55**
Canon Pyon, **66**
Ewyas Harold, **99**
Garway, **36**
Kilpeck, **57**

Ledbury, 39, 41
   St. Catherine's Chapel, **122**
Madley, **130**
Pembridge, **112**
Peterstow, **178**

HERTFORDSHIRE

Hemel Hempstead, 40

HUNTINGDONSHIRE

Great Paxton, 25, 26, 32, 33, 37

St. Neot's, 15, **18**

KENT

Barfreston, **34**, 37, **39**, 46, 48, **59**, 68
Canterbury—
   St. Martin's, 17, 18, 19
   SS. Pancras & Mary, 19, 20, 22
   SS. Peter & Paul, 19, 22
Chartham, **109**

Lydd, 20, 26
Rainham, 12, 44, 47
Reculver, 17, 19, 20, 26, 40
St. Margaret's at Cliffe, 41, **43**, **44**
Westwell, **77**

LANCASHIRE

Halsall, **123**

LEICESTERSHIRE

Hallaton, 12, **97**

North Kilworth, **102**

LINCOLNSHIRE

Barton-on-Humber, **22**, 26
Boston St. Botolph's, 71, 72, 78, **110**
Brant Broughton, **149**
Cotes-by-Stow, **69**
Gedney, **17**
Grantham, 65, **128**
Heckington, 68, 70, 71, **117, 118**
Long Sutton, **177**
Louth, 6, **7**

Moulton, **11, 64**
Mumby, **89**
Northorpe, **106**
Sleaford, **129**
Stow, 25, 41
Threckingham, **95**
Weston, **84**
Whaplode, 41, 54

MONMOUTHSHIRE

Chepstow, **16**, 48
Newport St. Woolos, **50**

Penhow, **91**
Wentlooge, **169**

NORFOLK

Attleborough, **175**
Aylsham, **127**
Blakeney, **10**, 15, 63
Cawston, **174**
Cley, 73, **152**
Elsing, 70
Forncett St. Peter, **28**
Holme Hale, **90**

Snettisham, 70, **115**
Swaffham, **173**
Tilney All Saints, 41, 54, **73**
Walsoken, **3**, 39, 41, 44, **49**, 56
West Walton, **4**, 9, 13, 58, 59, 60, 63, 64, **80, 81, 82, 94, 105**
Wiggenhall St. Mary V., **136**

NORTHAMPTONSHIRE

Barnack, **24, 25, 33**, 59
Brixworth, **2**, 14, 20, 21, 25, **26**, 26, 29, 30, **34**, 66
Castor, **1**, 42
Earl's Barton, 24, **27**, 27, 30, **32**, 41
Lowick, **148**

Middleton Cheney, **104**
Northampton St. Peter's, 39, 41, 43
Polebrook, 59, 63, **71**
Wakerley, **53**, 56
Warmington, 59, 62, 65, 71, 83

NORTHUMBERLAND

Hexham, 23, 26
Norham, **45**

Rothbury, **75**

NOTTINGHAMSHIRE

Hawton, 70, **121, 133**

OXFORDSHIRE

Adderbury, 6, 58, 75, **132**
Bloxham, 71, 73, 82, **163**
Chinnor, **108**
Cuddesdon, 10, 40, 54, **68**
Ducklington, **47, 48**
Iffley, 39, 42, 46, 47, 49

Minster Lovell, **142**
South Newington, **8**, 78
Stanton Harcourt, 58, 63, 75
Thame, 6, 79, **83**
Witney, 13, 55, 70, 83, **96**

RUTLAND

Whissendine, **114**

SHROPSHIRE

Much Wenlock, 14, 39, 42

SOMERSET

Athelney, 23, 25
Batcombe, **172**
Crowcombe, 82, **141**

Isle Abbots, **180**
Kingston on the Quantocks, **143**
Timberscombe, **165**

SUFFOLK

Cavendish, 82, **150**
Dennington, **131**
Hoxne, **170**
Kersey, 82, **153**
Lavenham, 15, 79, **145**

Little Saxham, 40, **42**
Southwold, 82, **140**
Stoke by Nayland, **146**
Wingfield, **124**

SUSSEX

Battle, **63**
Broadwater, **15**
Bury, **12**, 63
Clymping, 40, **41**, 68

Etchingham, **107**
Sompting, 32, 33, 37
Worth, 12, 25, 26, 29, 32

WILTSHIRE

Bradford-on-Avon, 26, 27, 29

Edington, 78, **134**

WORCESTERSHIRE

Evesham St. Laurence, **161**

Ripple, 54, **103**

YORKSHIRE

Adel, **35**, 37, 48, 49, **54**, 56, **62**
Barton-le-Street, **51**
Beverley St. Mary, 70, **125**, **139**
Birkin, **38**, 58
Filey, 58, **76**
Fishlake, **137**

Hedon, **126**
Hull Holy Trinity, 15, 70, 85, **111**
Kirk Hammerton, **21**
Patrington, **5**, 70, 71, 78, **116**, **119**, **120**
Tickhill, 15, **19**
Welwick, **138**

WALES

FLINTSHIRE

Mold, **162**

RADNORSHIRE

Old Radnor, **147**

GENERAL INDEX

Aconbury, 100
Adderbury, 6, 58, 75, 132
Adel, 35, 37, 48, 49, 54, 56, 62
Adwalton, 63
Aisles, 11, 26, 39, 54, 58, 70
Alberbury, 40
Alme, 49
Almondbury, 85
Angels, carved, 84
Arcades, 9, 41, 53, 72
Arches—
    Anglo-Norman, 31-32
    Decorated, 72
    Early English, 60
    Four-centred, 78
    Late Norman, 55-56
    Norman, 43
    Perpendicular, 82
    Pointed, 51, 56
    Pre-Conquest, 27-28
    Transitional, 66
Ashburton, 82, 144
Askham Bryan, 14
Astley, 43
Athelney, 23, 25
Attleborough, 175
Avebury, 29
Aylsham, 127

Bampton, 47
Barford St. Michael, 40
Barfreston, 34, 37, 39, 46, 48, 59, 68
Barnack, 24, 25, 33, 59
Barnsley, Glos., 29
Barton-le-Street, 51
Barton-on-Humber, 22, 26
Base courses, 9, 59, 72, 81, 170
Batcombe, 172
Battle, 63
Bay design, 13, 42-43
Bede, Venerable, 16, 18, 19, 20, 21, 22
Beeston next Mileham, 11
Berkswell, 43
Berrynarbor, 62
Beverley St. Mary, 70, 125, 139
Bibury, 10, 27, 29, 68
Bicester, 25
Birkin, 38, 58
Bishop Auckland, 65, 98

Bishop's Cleeve, 9, 13, 40, 55
Bishopstone, 26
Blakeney, 10, 15, 63
Blockley, 38, 56
Bloxham, 71, 73, 82, 163
Blundeston, 70
Blythburgh, 14
Boarhunt, 32
Bosbury, 54
Bosham, 32, 33
Boston St. Botolph's, 71, 72, 78, 110
Bracebridge, 26
Bradford-on-Avon, 26, 27, 29
Bradninch, 179
Bradwell-on-Sea, 19, 20, 22
Brant Broughton, 149
Brayton, 55
Breamore, 25
Bredon, 40, 54, 55
Brimpsfield, 14, 47
Bristol St. James', 46
Britford, 25
Brixworth, 2, 14, 20, 21, 25, 26, 26, 29, 30, 34, 66
Broadwater, 15
Buckland, 58
Building crafts—
    Carpentry, 74, 85
    Carving, 49, 53, 56, 76-77, 84
    Masonry, 6, 53, 77, 83
Building materials, 6, 17, 18, 26-27, 37, 81
Buildwas, 56
Burgh, 61
Bury, 12, 63
Buttresses—
    Decorated, 72
    Early English, 59
    Norman, 43
    Perpendicular, 86
    Transitional, 67

Caerleon, 17
Cambridge St. Mary the Great, 155
Canon Pyon, 66
Canterbury—
    St. Martin, 17, 18, 19
    SS. Pancras & Mary, 19, 20, 22
    SS. Peter & Paul, 19, 22

Capitals—
  Decorated, 73
  Early English, 61
  Late Norman, 55
  Norman, 45
  Perpendicular, 84
  Pre-Conquest, 28, 33
  Transitional, 66
Carving, *see* Ornament
Castle Ashby, 14
Castle Hedingham, 46, 54, 68
Castle Rising, 47
Castleacre, 15
Castles, Norman, 35-36
Castor, **1**, 42
Cavendish, 82, **150**
Cawston, **174**
Celtic influence, 18-19, 21, 22, 49
Chantry chapels, 69, 81
Charlbury, 12
Charlton-on-Otmoor, 78
Chartham, **109**
Chedgrave, 40
Cheltenham, 74
Chepstow, **16**, 48
Cherry Hinton, 60, 61, 63, 68
Chiddingfold, 12
Chinnor, **108**
Chipping Campden, 15
Chipping Norton, 74
Cholsey, 14, 41
Church builders—
  Celtic, 18, 21
  Imitation of Roman examples, 16-17, 23
  Mediæval, 5-6, 15
  Norman, 37-38
  St. Augustine, 19
Cirencester, **6**
Claverley, 40
Clee, 30
Clerestories, 11
  Decorated, 71
  Early English, 58
  Norman, 40
  Perpendicular, 81
Cley, 73, **152**
Clifton Reynes, **151**, **164**
Clymping, 40, **41**, 68
Cockfield, 12
Colchester, Holy Trinity, 28
Cold Aston, 47
Coltishall, 29
Columns, *see* Piers—
  Late Norman, 55
  Norman, 44
  Pre-Conquest, 28
Compton, 41
Condover, 68
Contracts, building, 6
Corbels and corbel tables, 42, 59
Corbridge, 22, 25

Cotes-by-Stow, **69**
Cotterstock, 65
Cranworth, 29
Crewkerne, 15
Crowcombe, **141**
Cruciform churches, *see* Planning
Cuckmer, 46
Cuddesdon, 10, 40, 54, **68**
Culbone, 29
Cullompton, 85, **160**, **176**
Curvilinear tracery, 73

DAGLINGWORTH, 29, 30
Darlington, 64
Decorated style, 69-75
  Transition to Perpendicular, 76
Deerhurst, 26, 30, **30**
Dennington, **131**
Documents, 6
Doorways, 14
  Decorated, 73
  Early English, 61
  Late Norman, 55
  Norman, 47-48
  Perpendicular, 82-83
  Pre-Conquest, 29-30
  Transitional, 66
Dover, 25, 44
Downton, 58
Ducklington, **47**, **48**
Durham, 31, 56

EARL'S BARTON, 24, 27, **27**, 30, **32**, 41
Early English style, 57-64
  Transition to Decorated, 65
Easington, **52**
Eaton Bray, 63, **85**, **86**, **87**, **92**
Edington, 78, **134**
Eglwys Cwm, 25
Elkstone, 47, 49, **60**
Elm, 58
Elsing, 70
Emneth, 54
Enford, 44
Enstone, 59
Escomb, **20**, 21
Etchingham, **107**
Evesham St. Laurence, **161**
Ewelme, 14
Ewerby, 71
Ewyas Harold, **99**

FARINGDON, 54, **67**, **72**
Farmington, 10
Farndish, **88**
Figure sculpture, 49, 56, 61, 84
Filey, 58, **76**

Fingest, 40
Fishlake, 137
Fontmell Magna, 168
Fordington, 49
Forncett St. Peter, 28
Frampton, 59

Garsington, 55
Garway, 36
Geddington, 27
Gedney, 17
Glastonbury, 18
Gloucester Cathedral, 76, 80
Gooderstone, 74
Grantham, 65, 128
Great Baddow, 171
Great Bedwin, 55
Great Dunham, 26, 27
Great Missenden, 113
Great Paxton, 25, 26, 32, 33, 37
Great Rollright, 78
Great Yarmouth, 65
Great Yeldham, 14
Greenstead, 18
Grosmont, 62
Guilds, 80

Haddiscoe, 46
Hadstock, 37
Hallaton, 12, 97
Halsall, 123
Hampnet, 42, 47
Hampton Poyle, 78
Handborough, 49, 59
Hanslope, 43
Hanwell, 73
Hartlepool, 58, 64
Hartwell, 87
Hawton, 70, 121, 133
Heckington, 68, 70, 71, 117, 118
Hedon, 126
Hemel Hempstead, 40
Hempstead, 14
Hexham, 23, 26
Heydon, 11
Highworth, 49
Hillesden, 157
Holme Hale, 90
Horsham, 58, 64
Hoxne, 170
Hull Holy Trinity, 15, 70, 85, 111
Hunstanton, 74

Ickleton, 26, 28, 32, 33
Iffley, 39, 42, 46, 47, 49
Isle Abbots, 180
Ivinghoe, 63

Jarrow, 21

Kersey, 82, 153
Ketton, 71
Kilpeck, 57
King's Sutton, 83
Kingston on the Quantocks, 143
Kirk Hammerton, 21

Lambourne, 54
Langford, 26, 31, 32
Launceston, 158
Lavenham, 15, 79, 145
Ledbury, 39, 41
    St. Catherine's Chapel, 122
Leek, 74
Leicester St. Nicholas, 41
Leominster, 45
Little Coxwell, 62
Little Faringdon, 70, 74
Little Saxham, 40, 42
Little Walsingham, 11
Little Wratting, 48
Llanrychwy, 25
Long Melford, 15
Long Sutton, 177
Louth, 6, 7
Lowick, 148
Ludgershall, 73
Lullington, 43
Lydd, 20, 26
Lyminge, 19

Madley, 130
Madron, 25
Maids Moreton, 156
Malinslee, 47
Malton, 75
Mapledurham, 12
Melbourne, 40, 46
Mendlesham, 75
Merton, 78
Middleton Cheney, 104
Minster-in-Thanet, 41
Minster Lovell, 142
Mold, 162
Monkwearmouth, 21, 22, 25, 27, 29, 31
Morwenstow, 14
Mouldings—
    Decorated, 72, 73
    Early English, 61, 66
    Illustrations, 88
    Late Norman, 55
    Norman, 44, 48
    Pre-Conquest, 30
Moulton, 11, 64
Mowsley, 65
Much Wenlock, 14, 39, 42
Mumby, 89

NANTWICH, 78
Nateley, 68
Newport St. Woolos, **50**
New Romney, 41
New Shoreham, 40
Newton, 26, 68
Norham, **45**
Northampton St. Peter, 40, 41, 43
North Cerney, **79**
North Kilworth, **102**
Northleach, 83, **154**
North Leigh, 26
Northmoor, 14
Northorpe, **106**
Norton, Co. Durham, 14
Notgrove, 47
Nottingham St. Mary's, 15

OCKHAM, 63
Old Radnor, **147**
Ornament, 24
 Decorated, 73
 Early English, 61
 Norman, 48-49, 52
 Perpendicular, 81, 83, 84
 Transitional, 56
Overbury, 41
Oxford—
 Cathedral Latin Chapel, 4
 Merton College Chapel, 4
 New College Chapel, 4
 St. Giles, 4
 St. Mary Magdalene, 72
 St. Mary's, 14

PAIGNTON, 48
Parapets, 71, 72, 81
Patrington, 5, 70, 71, 78, **116, 119, 120**
Patrixbourne, 40
Pembridge, **112**
Penhow, **91**
Perpendicular style, 79-88
Perranzabuloe, 25
Peterstow, **178**
Piers—
 Decorated, 73
 Early English, 60, 66
Pittington, 41
Plans, church—
 Decorated, 70
 Early English, 57-58, 65
 Illustrations, 8
 Late Norman, 54
 Norman, 38-40
 Perpendicular, 81
 Pre-Conquest, 24-26
Polebrook, 59, 63, **71**
Polstead, 44

Porches, 13, 22
 Decorated, 71
 Early English, 59
 Late Norman, 54
 Norman, 40
 Perpendicular, 82-84
Potterne, 58

QUENINGTON, 49

RAINHAM, 12, 44, 47
Ramsey, 54
Rayleigh, **159**
Reculver, 17, 19, 20, 26, 40
Redbourne, 42
Repton, 25, 26, 28, 31, **31**, 33
Rewe, **167**
Ripon, 26
Ripple, 54, **103**
Roman influence, 3, 16-18, 20, 22
Romano-British churches, 3-4, 17-18
Roofs—
 Decorated, 71, 74-75
 Early English, 62
 Norman, 49-50
 Perpendicular, 85
Rothbury, **75**
Ryton, **101**

ST. ALBAN'S St. Michael, 41
St. Augustine, 4, 19
St. Germans, 40
St. Gwithian, 25
St. Margaret's at Cliffe, 41, **43, 44**
St. Mary le Wigford, 63
St. Neot's, 15, **18**
St. Wilfred, 23, 25, 26
Sandiacre, 72
Saxon period, styles of building in, 16-30
 Transition to Norman, 31
Saxthorpe, 14, 41
Shelton, 14
Shifnal, 13, 40, 70
Shottesbrooke, 70
Shrewsbury St. Mary's, 54, 55
Silchester, 17, 20, 22
Sleaford, **129**
Slimbridge, **93**
Snettisham, 70, **115**
Soham, **65**
Somerford Keynes, 30
Sompting, 32, 33, 37
South Lopham, 29, 41
South Newington, **8**, 78
Southwold, 82, **140**

Spires, 59, 66, 71, 86
Stamford All Saints, 63
　St. Mary, 71
Stanton Harcourt, 58, 63, 75
Stanton St. John, 68
Stanton St. Quintin, 40
Steetley, 37
Stewkley, 39
Steyning, 41
Stoke by Nayland, 146
Stottesdon, 41
Stow, 25, 41
Studland, 37
Styles, naming of, 4
Sutton, Cambridgeshire, 78, 79, 135
Sutton Courtney, 56
Sutton St. Mary, 41, 59
Swaffham, 173
Swalcliffe, 41
Swymbridge, 166

Tamworth, 12, 14
Thame, 6, 79, 83
Threckingham, 95
Tickhill, 15, 19
Tilney All Saints, 41, 54, 73
Timberscombe, 165
Torquay, Tor Hill, 25
Tostock, 11
Towers, 13-14, 22
　Decorated, 71
　Early English, 58, 65
　Late Norman, 55
　Norman, 40-42
　Perpendicular, 86
　Pre-Conquest, 25, 33
Tracery, 66, 73-74, 77, 82
Transepts, 25, 39, 54, 58, 65, 70
Transition—
　Decorated to Perpendicular, 76
　Early English to Decorated, 65
　Norman to Early English, 51
　Saxon to Norman, 31
Tredington, 48
Tunsted, 75
Tydd St. Giles, 59

Uffington, 13, 14, 58, 78

Vestries, 40

Wakerley, 53, 56
Wall arcading, see under Walls
Walls—
　Decorated, 72
　Early English, 59
　Norman, 42
　Perpendicular, 81
　Pre-Conquest, 26-27
Walsoken, 3, 39, 41, 44, 49, 56
Waltham, 33
Wareham, 32
Warkworth, 38
Warmington, 59, 62, 65, 71, 83
Water Eaton, 14
Wells, 60
Welwick, 138
Wentlooge, 169
Westminster Abbey, 33, 37
Weston, 84
West Tarring, 64
West Walton, 4, 9, 13, 58, 59, 60, 63, 64,
　80, 81, 82, 94, 105
Westwell, 77
Whaplode, 41, 54
Whissendine, 114
Wiggenhall St. Mary V., 136
Willersey, 11, 14
Windows—
　Decorated, 73
　Early English, 60, 67
　Glazing, 53, 77
　Late Norman, 55
　Norman, 45-47, 53, 67
　Perpendicular, 81-82
　Pre-Conquest, 28-29, 66
　Transitional, 66-68
Windrush, 61
Wing, 21, 23, 26, 31, 32
Wingfield, 124
Witney, 13, 55, 70, 83, 96
Wittering, 28, 32, 33
Womerton, 41
Woodstock, 61
Wootton Wawen, 25
Worth, 12, 25, 26, 29, 32
Worth Matravers, 43
Wroxeter, 38, 41

Printed in Great Britain at The Darien Press, *Edinburgh*